The Truth is a Lie

Behind the Scenes of the Family Court System

Indy GoHard

Copyright © 2022

All Rights Reserved

Dedication

Dedicated to all the honest, hardworking, and loving parents who have been abused by the family court system. In this book, you will see examples of how Judges and court-appointed child representatives treated me in two separate high-conflict cases and how their oversight, negligence, and misconduct lead to the detriment of families through the hands of manipulative and bitter co-parents who claim to be innocent in these cases. For those who have suffered the aftermath of domestic violence, parental alienation, suicide, murder, and those who may be going through the many dimensions of family court today, you are not alone.

-Indy GoHard

This book is based on real events I experienced in the family court system, along with brief descriptions of other related cases. I am not an attorney, legal advisor, or clinical professional. The information in this book is from experience, research, education, and common sense. Certain names were altered to protect the identity of the accused.

Acknowledgment

Everyone mentioned here has either helped me directly or indirectly. Each person is either an essential part of my growth or has helped me when I needed support. Thank you all, for all you are to me.

God, Arvion Webb, Jo'Vanni Smith, Londyn Ford, Prince Ford, Joshua Toler, Yolande Roseley, Clarence Brown, Ivonne Wilson, Jeffrey Wilson, Annette McDuffey, Ronlitta Sylvester, Nicole Keys, Tiffany Fusilier, Chatara McClain, Marshalena Smith, Carlotta Knight, Amanda Ferguson, Tera Toler, Lisa Chastain, Denise Defour, Amanda Bolton, Ashley Mikhaylov, Brett Cremeens, Oprah Winfrey, Iyanla Vanzant, April Mason, and Love Dorsey.

Contents

Dedication iii

Acknowledgment iv

Preface vi

Chapter 1 The Bitter Deceiver 1

Chapter 2 Moving On – The timeline 8

Chapter 3 Child Support Court 16

Chapter 4 The Custody Battle 23

Chapter 5 The Guardian Ad Litem 30

Chapter 6 Maternal Instincts 37

Chapter 7 My Sister's Keeper 53

Chapter 8 A Long Road Ahead 63

Chapter 9 The Manipulative Deceiver 67

Chapter 10 The Beginning of The End 78

Chapter 11 The Great Escape 86

Final Thoughts 100

About the Author 102

Preface

Parental alienation syndrome is a psychological condition when abusive parents and relatives choose to disconnect children from their other parents and family members out of spite. It has become a mental health crisis due to its lasting effects on children and the impacted parent. In this book, you will learn about events that led up to the kidnapping of four-day-old Kayden Powell, taken from his bassinette in 2014 by his half-aunt Kristen Smith, how I was connected to this case, and how a Colorado court completely ignored cries for help concerning her which would have prevented the situation altogether. I will also discuss how the courts determine who is awarded custody in high-conflict cases, how they treat protective parents who seek refuge for their children and themselves, how I entered family court a second time, and how I was able to escape with my two youngest children using the law against court rules.

The Truth is a Lie

Chapter 1
The Bitter Deceiver

I met the Bitter Deceiver in 2004. He was 18, and I was 19. Early in the relationship, he decided to go to college out of state. We agreed we would remain together through long distance. I was in Jr. college for business and aspired to become a businesswoman. After he left, and as time went on, distance grew between us. Of course, we were young, and I was in a different headspace. I already had a 3-year-old child; he was free, single, and disengaged in a whole other state. I did not want to set the expectation that he would be there for my son and me in the long run, so I decided it would be best for us to split. The feeling was not mutual, and after about six months of being away, the Bitter Deceiver moved back to Denver so we could be together.

I was living with my grandmother, and he was living with his mother. My family adored him, and I got along with most of his. Even though it was not the ideal situation, from growing up in a toxic atmosphere, my longing to establish and maintain a loving, close nit family has always been something sought after. This family dynamic was never demonstrated to either one of us. We were two teenagers trying to have an adult experience the best way we understood. Since I already had a child, life started for me early. I was ready to lock down and generate a blueprint for the future with my so-called "life partner." He gave me his word that he wanted the same things. He never really showed it in his actions, but the boy talked a good game.

About a year and a half into our relationship, I became pregnant after moving into a townhome together. At this point, I shifted my career interest to radio and television and attended the Ohio Center for Broadcasting towards the end of 2005. I was about to be 21 years old at this time. In between me going to school and on the way to becoming a mother of two, I would catch the Bitter Deceiver in little unnecessary lies. He was also easily triggered to anger. On good days, he would have all these grandiose ideas on how he could make money, which was mostly multi-level marketing jobs like selling cologne in grocery store parking lots or activity books for kids. He would be gone all day, sometimes bringing home between ten and thirty bucks daily, and was very proud of it. As you can imagine, this caused an extreme rift in how I viewed the direction of our relationship because it became evident he really did not know what he wanted to do with his life, he wasn't nearly as motivated or ambitious as I was, and our pending and growing bills were not enough to get him to do more. I should have noticed this when he decided to quit school and return to Denver because "ain't no way I was gonna stop going after my dream for someone I barely knew." But we think we know everything at this age.

The Truth is a Lie

The moment I realized our relationship was not going to work was on the day of my graduation, October 25, 2006. Despite his impeccable lip service and our unexplained love for each other, we just did not work. Our daughter was six months old at the time, and we just received a notice to vacate the townhome on this very day. His family and some of my family gathered at the Olive Garden to celebrate my commencement. When I arrived, the Bitter Deceiver was sitting across the table with our baby, and I noticed that he had his cell phone under the table texting. Our baby was crying, and I got annoyed because he was not paying attention to her and to make matters worse, he forgot her binky and her bottle.

So, I said, "hey… Bitter Deceiver… our baby is crying, and maybe we should try figuring out how to console her." He rudely replies, "I don't know what you're tripping about. Everything has been going your way all day." After he made that statement, extreme anger overcame me, and I left everyone at the table. He came chasing behind to insult and argue with me in the parking lot, not considering earlier that day; I was all in a tizzy about the thought of being evicted, and as a man, he was not in any position, nor did he attempt to do anything about it. Shortly after that, we split, and he ended up getting a real job at the airport and then a tire place. This didn't change how I felt though. The Bitter Deceiver was never in my hair about how our daughter was being raised, and we never had any issues as it concerned her. Our co-parenting relationship was the typical baby momma, baby daddy surface-level drama, but our focus was completely on taking care of her. The following year, we tried working it out for the sake of our child and my son. His family accepted my son as their own, and they were very good to him.

Not too long after we got back together, he decided to enlist in the military with the intention of getting government assistance and free education. At the time, he claimed he wanted to be a mechanic of some sort and aspired to be in a financial position to care for our child. When he was finally able to contact me from bootcamp, we discussed taking our relationship to the next step and getting married.

He was stationed in Norfolk, Virginia give or take August 2008. I could not fathom the idea of leaving my aging grandmother back in Denver. But once again, we tried working out our relationship long distance. My desire to be on television and radio was put to rest after realizing how closed of a market Colorado was. My dream was to create sound bites for movies, write movie scripts, produce music for video games, comedy skits, and interview celebrities. I did not have the right mentors or resources to make the right connections for the type of audience I wanted to attract. Social media was in its baby stages and had limited functionality. Video uploads and online marketing strategies were not even a big thing yet, so I ended up in the world of finance and got a gig at a bank one year before he left for the military.

The Truth is a Lie

When the Bitter Deceiver came back from tour and was able to visit for a few days, he presented me with a 1.5-carat diamond ring and asked me to marry him. I said yes. But again, our relationship was not strong. I had my doubts, still holding onto the past and the reason I broke up with him in the first place. I still couldn't imagine the thought of leaving my grandmother, and every time we had an opportunity to talk, he was always highlighting the financial benefits of us being married once he joined. I felt as though he wanted to marry me for transactional purposes and not for love and genuine building.

About a month after he left, I noticed interactions between the Bitter Deceiver and this young lady while surfing MySpace. I reached out to her inquiring about their relationship and how they knew one another. In other words, I came to her "as a woman." She told me about a time they spent together at a hotel having sex all day and how he proclaimed to be this top-notch businessman with his shit together. As I recall the moment, I remember the lie he told me. Check this out…. He said he was going to meet some "homies" at a hotel to play video games; I just knew that it was complete bullshit.

Thinking back, hours after he left, I remember my stomach being in knots, and when I tried to reach him by phone, it would go straight to voicemail. I knew what was up. Growing up, being the only girl with two brothers and a cousin who is like my brother taught me a lot about unevolved men (no offense). When the Bitter

INDY GOHARD

Deceiver came to see me later that evening, he did not touch or kiss me, thank God. I do not remember the excuse he gave as to why he couldn't be reached, but his actions after the fact, plus his bogus story earlier that day, confirmed everything I needed from her side. Moreover, I hacked his myspace account, where I found all the receipts. One of his security questions asked for the name of his first pet, so I asked him what it was, and the man actually told me, lol!

What made me view him differently was she was literally just celebrating her 18th birthday. We were already 20 and 21 when he cheated with her. The fact that he deceived the young lady, and the reality that she was 17 when they had sex, made me think of how many other young ladies he may have done this with and if he was out here having sex with underage girls. Around the third year of our relationship, we would argue about his desire to solicit women for services. Circling back to his work patterns, he would be gone all day with nothing to show, but he was always happy. It made absolutely no sense to me, and I chalked it up as him just being a little slow. A lot of things he did, did not make natural sense, and we bumped heads a lot. Once I got this revelation, the thoughts running through my mind made me sick to my stomach for about a week. These were just my thoughts. He is the only one who knows what was really going on with him during that time, but I bet I am not too far off.

The Truth is a Lie

The first chance I received, I wrote him a "Dear John" letter ending our relationship for good. The engagement ring he gave me was later returned to him, and I remained single. Co-parenting was smooth. He set up an allotment in the amount of two hundred and sixty dollars each month for the benefit of our child. I guess that's something like child support when you're in the military. When he would come home to visit, our daughter would spend all her time with him until he returned to his station. She was still a baby and not in school yet. This dynamic carried on for two years, and in between visits with him, our daughter spent a lot of time with his mother. There was never any resistance between his family and me when they wanted to spend time with her. I got along with his mother and extended family. His sister and I never really saw eye-to-eye, but there was never resistance with her either. Everything was very simple.

Chapter 2
Moving On – The timeline

In July 2010, over two years after calling off the engagement, I decided to enter back into the dating scene. In February 2011, I was laid off from my job at the bank after serving three and a half years and started attending church to gain a little faith. After a couple of weeks of attending church with my father, I met my now ex-husband, who was the new drummer of the church. He will be referenced as Manipulative Deceiver later in this book, but to keep the integrity and flow of this story, he will be referenced as my husband since that's what he was during this time.

In July 2011, my daughter's aunt was getting married. The Bitter Deceiver and his family were made aware of my new relationship about a month prior, and we were invited to her wedding. My daughter was the flower girl. My soon-to-be husband arrived about an hour into the reception after he got off work. He and the Bitter Deceiver were introduced, acquainted, and had a conversation. I thought everything was cool. I was sitting in the reception hall with my back towards the door. A short moment later, I felt the sensation of warm hands gripping my shoulders from behind and whispering behind my head, "I got everything handled." At first, I thought it was my man, but when I looked the right of me, I saw it was not. I immediately got an attitude because I felt a lot of petty energy coming from him. We are at his sister's wedding, he grabs the back of my shoulders and whispers to me in front of my new man, and to top it off he tells me he had everything handled when there was no situation to be handled. What was that all about?

According to my new man, the Bitter Deceiver advised him not to marry me as he had concerns for our daughter's safety and he did not know him well enough to feel comfortable around her, he said we barely knew each other to be discussing marriage, and he also made sure to include that he was a sharpshooter in the military. I'm sure you could guess the relevance of why he would say that. At this time, our child was 5, and there were no true safety concerns relating to our children, as far as I could see, as it related to my new relationship. The only thing I was nervous about was my new man's drinking problem and the fact that he was not allowed to drive, but he was also in a program to get help. This was something the Bitter Deceiver was not made aware of, and being 25 years old, I didn't understand the severity of alcoholism since that wasn't something we ever dealt with in our relationship. Although I grew up knowing substance abusers, I was still very ignorant of the disease and the societal issues around it.

I considered we were only together for five months when discussing marriage, but my new man claimed he did not want us to move in together as boyfriend and girlfriend. He called it "shacking up." I was advised that "shacking up" was not an ideal living arrangement in the Christian Community, so we had talks about marriage before moving in together. I considered the only reason the Bitter Deceiver would even think my new man was a safety concern was that I suspected him of praying on and soliciting younger women when we were together. Why would he think I would even choose to be with someone like that? Maybe he had the foresight and saw signs that I still wasn't aware of after dealing with him. Who knows?

Let me take you back a little. Around April 2011, myself and the Bitter Deceiver discussed possibly sending the children to Virginia to be with him for a little while. Keep in mind the Bitter Deceiver was not aware of my relationship because of its newness. When he finally met my new man 3 months later at his sister's wedding and saw how serious we were about being together, the Bitter Deceiver became adamant about taking the children back to Virginia and proposed the idea that sending them would give me time to find stable employment since recently being laid off and would give him an opportunity to be with the children. Harmless and thoughtful, right?

My grandmother stressed the fact that in her culture, nobody moved out of the home until they were married, and she wanted me to hold strong to those beliefs despite the fact I already had two children out of wedlock. In the summer of 2011, I would leave my children in my grandmother's care as an added protection to not just bring anyone around them right away. For the two months this lasted, I went back home to see them for a while and then off again before she started fussing at me. In my opinion, sending them at that time would have been ideal as I was trying to find stable employment, wanting to gracefully move on with my life, get my children from being with her all the time, and made an innocent assumption the Bitter Deceiver had all good intentions.

Although I was in between jobs, my new man and I managed to get approved for an apartment. The apartment would not be ready until August 2011, so we moved into my father's place after my man's lease was up in June. My grandma was very vocal regarding her feelings about the direction I was headed in. She did not take into consideration for the past almost three years, I was single and focused. All I did was work and attend school. But I was naive to the world and the ways of society for being sheltered and then sheltering myself as an adult. I didn't even watch television, and when the news started affecting my perception of the world, I stopped watching that also. I am not saying I did not have a good time. I had a handful of friends I would hang with, and then it was back to business. I just wanted to live my life and did not want to live it alone or give up on love. Even though it was never demonstrated, my belief in true love is prevalent because true love is within me. And I knew if I had it, other people did too.

INDY GOHARD

Growing up, I did not understand why my parents or other family members stayed together in their chaos, nor did I understand why my grandmother chose to stay single after my grandfather left, but I simply chose neither. As a result of my core beliefs, my reality is I'm on baby daddy number 2 and entertaining a new relationship. Shit!! My logic was not allowing my children to grow up in chaos or permitting them to witness or endure abuse of any kind. In the midst of that, I also don't want to be an old lady who lost herself and decided against having a companion. My grandmother wanted me to work it out with the Bitter Deceiver, but she and nobody else was made aware of the true reason we broke up until now. Okay, back to the story….

After we moved in with my father in June, we were approved for the apartment in July, and we found out that we were pregnant with baby number 3. Nobody knew this. I was a few weeks pregnant when they met at the wedding to tie it all together. We both understood we would be crucified by the church and our families for moving so fast and not being married, so we kept the pregnancy news to ourselves. The initial plan for the children leaving was that The Bitter Deceiver's mother was going with them, so with that in mind, knowing the children were safe and with a trusted adult, I decided to send them. The only reason I considered sending my son was that their family played a huge part in his life, his biological father wasn't around, and I didn't want my children to be separated for one year. Both children also wanted to be with him, I was in a brand-new relationship, and it just made sense to me to at least give it a try. I felt if the Bitter Deceiver were willing to help, I would take it, but my new man did not like the idea. Both children left on July 27, 2011, shortly after the wedding, and were to return the following year, in July 2012, with visits from me in between. That was the agreement.

In August 2011, right after my fiancé and I moved into our apartment, we married at the Justice of the Peace in Colorado Springs, Colorado. My husband's mother was our only witness. This news infuriated the Bitter Deceiver, and things started getting strange. The conditions of sending the children to Virginia were; if it did not work out, they would come back without hesitation. There were issues registering my son for school due to the Bitter Deceiver not being his natural father and needing proof of residency, so my son returned to Colorado on September 20, 2011. Exactly two months. After my son came home, everything about the Bitter Deceiver's intentions was under investigation. Amid me being married and him being in a new relationship, he still wanted to adopt and change my son's last name when I was under the assumption that we were co-parenting and no matter what, he would be there as a bonus male figure to him. His actions were so extreme they caused a rift in my marriage because "my now" husband believed the Bitter Deceiver, and I still had something going on. I put two and two together and concluded that with his "get rich quick" train of thought, he wanted to add my son as his legal dependent; this way, he could include my son in his GI Bill and receive benefits for him also.

Our daughter stayed in Virginia with her grandmother after my son returned home and she started Kindergarten. When the children left, the allotment was also stopped because, of course, now, she was in his care. Everything seemed to be going well. He was also in a new relationship. The girl was nice and easy to talk to at first. Then out of nowhere, they both teamed up against my husband and me and just talked mad shit about me being an unfit mother and questioning my parenting. I do not recall if she had any children of her own, but whatever she was doing to my baby's hair left 6 quarter size bald spots in her head that no one had any logical explanation for. After a short while, her grandmother and I made plans, and she returned home on December 15, 2011. She stayed only five months. When she returned, she came home with apparent abandonment issues and nightmares. She would cry when my husband left the house, even if he were to check the mail. When I bought this to his and his mother's attention, they both brushed it off like it was not a big deal and claimed she was fine. That Christmas, literally ten days after sending her back, he never called or sent her anything. Likewise, I found out; three out of the five months she was there, he was in Chicago attending school, which he never disclosed to me. If I had known, I would have never sent the children to begin with. They were sent because he said he wanted to be with them.

After my daughter returned home, the Bitter Deceiver's visiting schedule returned to the way it was before. He also ended the relationship with the girl he was dating. Once again, everything appeared to be okay "on the surface," but my husband began taking issue with the Bitter Deceiver. He noticed every time he would come into town to see our child, he would rent a car of the same make and model as mine or one that I said I wanted in the past. The Bitter Deceiver always had something slick to say about my husband when I would ask him for money for our child.

After she returned home, he would send the allotment whenever he wanted to and say things like, "You got a husband. Why are you asking me for money?" Two hundred and sixty dollars is not a lot of money. I felt that since he was this upstanding father like he claimed to be, despite whose household she was in, he would still help take care of her. Regardless of his situation and feelings, she is still his responsibility, and he was not being hit over the head in support of her. He just did not want to put money in my pockets so long as I was in a relationship with someone else. As a matter of fact, he swore I only wanted the money to support my new baby.

Chapter 3
Child Support Court

In 2012, I was finally over the drama that the Bitter Deceiver was bringing my way about this money every month, so I decided to sue him for child support. Regardless of the amount, since he was not physically and barely financially helping me support her, he should assume responsibility for her. The entire year of 2012 was mute, and we did not hear from the Bitter Deceiver. He did not reach out for her birthday and barely called to talk to her any other day. He also never expressed sharing physical custody after sending her back home. Around August 2012, he was just about to be discharged after 4 years in the military and was served with a subpoena right before he could disappear. Our first hearing was either in May or June 2012. He attended over the phone as he was still the property of the United States and was given the right to a paternity test before the final hearing. This gave him time to create a narrative that would influence the weak-minded and change everyone's life forever.

In January 2012, I found permanent employment and started working as a Foreclosure Specialist at a loan-serving company. My duties included managing a portfolio of homes in default status, headed towards foreclosure, and keeping investors aware of each property's processes. I often searched homeowners who abandoned their properties through a procedure called skip tracing. This helped the loan professionals communicate with the investors about a projected timeline and to see if a deal could be worked out between the investor and the homeowner. My husband was a professional cover band musician and drummer for various churches around town. He was preparing to produce a televised drumming competition called "Drum off Battle" and was filming a commercial pilot for the event. Everything "seemed" to be on the up and up as far as my marriage was concerned, I was about seven months along in my pregnancy, but I noticed it was eerily quiet. We had not heard from the Bitter Deceiver in months after the first hearing. The only time I was in contact with him was when my grandmother passed away in July. After that, not a peep.

Before the end of the year, his paternity was determined, and the final child support hearing was scheduled on January 28, 2013. It is now the week of January 20, 2013, about eight months after the first child support hearing, a week away from the final hearing, and still no word from the Bitter Deceiver. My husband and I were discussing our upcoming schedules. He said he needed to pick my daughter up early from school the day of January 31st because they needed to finish the commercial pilot for the drum show, and no one would be home when she got off the school bus.

January 28, 2013, the morning of the final child support court, on the way out the door, while taking the children to school, my kids noticed 3 flat tires and graffiti on my truck. The graffiti read, "stupid bitch, slut." Funny thing was the tires were not slashed. The air was let out. I recalled a time he explained how to release air from a tire without damaging it when he worked at the tire place. The spray paint was also removable. I believe it was sprayed with fake snow. I called in to report the damages around 7:00 am. Since there was no evidence of anyone damaging my vehicle, and video surveillance was not as popular back then, there was nothing the police could do. I didn't have enemies or friends who turned enemies, and I knew the Bitter Deceiver had something to do with it because it was done by someone who apparently had a conscious. A true enemy is going to make sure to stop the person they are targeting. Think about it. It's the day of the final child support hearing, and now my truck is vandalized. What a coincidence!

When we arrived at court that morning, he and this woman, who I believed was representing him gave each other a look as if they were surprised, I made it. Their body language was awkward, and I was served with a motion called Allocation of Parental Responsibilities. He brought concerns to the court that I was not allowing him to see our child and I was keeping her away from him. We were both ordered to attend a mediation hearing. At this hearing, he was ordered to pay one hundred twenty-seven dollars a month. This was based on his telling the court that he would be able to visit every other weekend. I was so confused because we hadn't heard from him, and why was he up here lying?

The Truth is a Lie

I have never been the type to keep my children from visiting with their other parents because they weren't paying child support. This is an issue that women, especially women of color, have been statistically known for and that I have factually seen with my own two eyes. But all of us are not the same, and the men who seek to persist in having their way with women who help them will use the court system to continue emotional and psychological abuse. I was a child in the family court system, and the importance of having my biological parents in my life was fundamental despite the chaos and dysfunction we experienced. We were blessed to have a caregiver who protected us against ignorance and stupidity "by all means necessary." Being given the cognitive opportunity to think for myself equipped me with the ability to decipher stability against instability and grounded me as a responsible adult.

January 31, 2013, was a normal morning. I got my babies dressed for school and waited with them at the bus stop before heading to work. I remember vividly giving my baby girl a big hug and kiss, telling her to be good, and don't let anyone play in her hair. I also let her know that her stepfather would be there to pick her up after school. She said, "ok, mommy, I love you too." Her bus pulled up, and my baby was on the school bus headed to school. I remember saying a little prayer in my head, "Lord, please keep my babies safe." Like I ritually did, and I headed to work.

INDY GOHARD

Around 2 pm, close to the end of school, I received a frantic call from my husband. He was upset because when he went to pick my daughter up from school, unbeknown to both of us, the Bitter Deceiver was in the office accompanied by a woman with papers and a picture of my child. He described this woman as the same person at the child support hearing three days prior. He told me they appeared to be in a relationship, and she didn't seem to represent him.

While in the school office with the Bitter Deceiver and this woman, my husband passed his phone to the Bitter Deceiver, and he asked me if it was okay if he could take our child for a few hours and return her. I told him, "No." Number one, I was unaware he was still in town. At court, he claimed he was immediately going back to Texas after the court hearing to handle some affairs." Furthermore, who was this woman he brought to the school, why does she have my child's personal information, and what is this information?" My thoughts, until this day, were that he planned to take our child out of school, hit the road back to Texas with him, begin a custody case in Texas, and leave me worried sick because my child would have never made it home off that school bus.

For all I knew, he could have been working on getting custody of her in Texas since he had already established residency there, and I would have had a different fight on my hands. I believe he intended to take my child and child support me. He was using his

The Truth is a Lie

wife in case anything went awry, and he could pass the blame on to her, which is exactly what ended up happening. The history of our relationship is telling. All the mess he was creating screamed; "Since we can't be together under the same roof, raising our children, I'm going to take our child, adopt your child, child support you, and now your husband, who I didn't want to marry you in the first place, will have to deal with that." Yes, petty and bitter people do things like that even after they have moved on. And yes, men can be petty and bitter too.

After declining the request of the Bitter Deceiver to take our daughter, he hands the phone back to my husband. Shortly after, I heard my husband yelling, "let her go, let her go! Let me call you back." The phone hangs up. He called me back out of breath and yelled, "that bitch took her, she grabbed her by the arm and threw her in the car, and they drove away!" According to the police statement, I called to report a child abduction at the school. An unknown woman with my ex has taken my child with his help. The officers contacted him by phone, and he confirmed with the dispatch that the woman who took our child was his wife, and they were visiting. He told them I usually give him a hard time seeing our child, and he wanted to visit her before they went back home to Texas. The officer said they sent text messages to my cell phone, but later I discovered they were purposely texting an old phone number and saying they were texting me. Of course, this was all for documentation's sake. There was no way the new number could be confused with the old one, and again, even if she was the one who texted me, I still didn't know anything about her! I never met her. I explained all this to the police, and due to the nature of the situation, no custody agreement, and proof that this woman was his legal wife, the officer's hands were tied, and there was nothing they could do but monitor the situation.

The officer advised the Bitter Deceiver to provide a time he would return our child since that wasn't established after he took her. Around 7 pm that evening, we met to exchange custody at the Aurora Municipal Center lobby. When I got my baby girl back, she was very quiet, and it appeared that she was just waking up from a nap. I asked her, "is everything okay?" She nodded yes. I asked her, "did you just wake up from a nap?" and she shook her head yes. I then walked to the kitchen to grab the plate I had made for her. It was hot wings, rice, and vegetables. When I placed the food on the table, I sat back down with her, and she began to cry. But she was acting so weird. I asked her, "did you have something to eat before you took a nap?" She quietly said yes. It was a brownie. At that point, my gut feeling painted a picture of her father and this woman, who I still don't know, giving her a sedative. But why would they do that? Was I over thinking this? Hmm... Let's keep going.

The Truth is a Lie

Chapter 4
The Custody Battle

The Bitter Deceiver was demanding full custody in his motion. Colorado is not a custody state. They go by a set of factors used to determine where a child will spend most of their time, and they calculate the child's financial support based on the number of overnights a parent has with the child. This is where the term "Allocation of Parental Responsibility" comes from. Because there are three hundred and sixty-five days in a year and the days cannot be divided equally, the person with the extra day in the fifty-fifty situation becomes the "primary custodial parent" and is given financial support from the "non-custodial parent" even though both parents technically share visitation and decision making equally "on paper." Whew!!

According to the Colorado Revised Statute, "The court shall determine the allocation of parental responsibilities, including parenting time and decision-making responsibilities, in accordance with the best interests of the child, giving PARAMOUNT CONSIDERATION to the child's safety and the physical, mental, and emotional conditions and needs of the child."

In February 2013, we moved from the apartment into a house. I did not inform the Bitter Deceiver of my move since I strongly suspected that he and his wife were responsible for the damage to my vehicle the morning of child support court the prior month.

I had no idea this motion existed because he sent it to my old apartment address, and as a result, I had no time to send a response back to the court. Since he filed this motion, we were ordered to attend a mediation hearing on April 13, 2013. The purpose of mediation is to collectively include an unbiased third-party opinion to help us conceive a plan for visitation since I objected his request for full custody. Why ask for full custody? Isn't that a bit extreme? At the hearing, we were ordered to exercise a visitation schedule every other weekend until we could devise a plan together.

In his motion, he told the court that I was jealous of his new wife and refused visitations with him, and it was all in someone else's handwriting, presumably, his wife's. There was no evidence that I refused visitations prior because he disappeared after leaving the military. This was never investigated. I didn't even know he had a wife and four stepchildren. But they believed this story as he highlighted his service in the military, which was looked at as noble and honorable in the sight of the court, there is no due process in family court, plus, black men were not fighting for their children in the legal system. Statistically, black men have been "popular for" leaving and abandoning their families. I theorized in the court's eye; this must have meant serious business for him. He argued that he left the military to return to be with our child. But how? He went straight to Texas after leaving the military and never told me. He said he "enlisted to provide financial stability for her and get free education!" But he wanted to marry me, provide a life for our child together, and he was upset he did not achieve his plan.

Furthermore, why didn't he give me the same courtesy to know his wife or even know he got married? Do I have a right to know who will be influencing my child? What is there to hide? And how exactly does the law define co-parenting?

From the timeline I provided, he was barely involved in her life due to his militant status. He only aggressively tried to be involved when he found out I was moving on with my life. When he was away, he didn't call to talk to her or even send her a single thing. It was his family who pitched in, not him. This was another issue. He believed that because his family was helping, it counted towards the personal relationship he should have built with his child. In my eyes, his family was doing exactly what any loving family would do, regardless of whether or not he was in the picture.

After the mediation hearing in April, my husband was on his way out the door and headed to work. I was lying in bed resting with our baby. My son was asleep upstairs in his room. A few moments later, my husband rushed back into the house extremely upset and yelling that someone had tried setting both our cars on fire at our new residence. When he examined the damage, he noticed liquid tracks in the cracks in the driveway leading to each car. He also noticed the gas doors on both vehicles were still locked. Imagine what it would have been like if we didn't have those locks? We just filled the gas tanks of both vehicles the night before. There was also a half-scorched sock that did not quite get enough momentum to burn through. The driver's side of my husband's car was a bit charred, and so was the passenger side of my truck. It looked like whoever did it tried opening the gas tanks but was unsuccessful. They poured gas in the cracks of the pavement, lit the sock on fire, threw it on the ground once they realized they could not get the gas tanks open, and took off without waiting to see if their plan were successful. One thing that stood out to me was my daughter was with her father's family when this happened. He was supposedly going back and forth between Texas, but I found out that he and his wife stayed with his sister for a short while. I'm not sure if he was there at the time of the incident, but what a great time to get rid of an entire family in a custody case, right? Plus, they both thought it was funny. Nobody else but us thought it was suspicious.

The Aurora Police Department was called, and when officers contacted them, their excuse was we just moved, and they didn't know where we lived. But they did because they could get my address from our daughter's registration information from her new school after we moved. They could easily track her in the centralized school system since we kept her in the same school district. This was the same way they were able to find my apartment when they kidnapped her from school and damaged my truck the first time. The administration did not have the option to hide a child's personal identifiable information from the other parent, especially since there was no court order hindering him from this information. After another run-in with damage done to both cars this time, I refused visitations with him despite the court order.

About a week after the hearing in April, I received a call from a detective at the Aurora Police Department. The Bitter Deceiver and his wife reported child abuse and neglect against me. When I got to the police precinct for questioning, he pulled up a photo of my daughter and her father together. He was holding her, and she had a bruise that covered about 20% of her back. After he showed this to me, I explained the recent crazy occurrences and the pending custody situation to the officer. Not only was this the first time I heard of this mysterious bruise, but I also never saw the bruise on her when they returned her to me. Also, the Bitter Deceiver was back and forth between Texas and Colorado and the last time he claimed to have seen her was in January when they took her from school. I looked at the photo and asked the detective to do a right click on the picture to check the details for the time and date it was taken. The date on the photo was January 31, 2013. The same day she was taken from school. After this discovery, the detective closed the case. So, my question was, was the bruise real? The only thing I could think to do at this point was document this.

One day in May 2013, the Bitter Deceiver and his wife wanted to talk to me. Mind you, during all the mess that was happening, I never formally met her. We chose the police precinct to meet. When I arrived, the Bitter Deceiver's wife introduced herself to me as "Kristen Smith." She asked me if I would have an issue with her picking up my daughter from school as if she wasn't the cause of all the mess that was happening. I noticed they were recording my response and told her, "No, because you kidnaped my daughter from school, and I don't like you." She said, "you don't know me," and I replied, "I don't need to."

Kristen had four children of her own. Not that it was any of my personal business, but I wondered how she could move around with her children like she was able to. It is not easy to travel between states with a family as large as theirs and as frequent as they had to keep up with their story. I assumed he was angry with me because I screwed up his plan to take our child back to Texas with him, and now he must move back to Colorado and show face to the court and his wife as if he has always been a father actively seeking a healthy relationship with our child. What a big fat front! Between January and June, they took several trips back to Texas. When they finally settled in Colorado, they were displaced and living at extended-stay hotels until they found a house to rent in Aurora, not too far from me.

The Truth is a Lie

Between May and June of 2013, our child still had not seen her father. The only time I could assume she did was when she was at his sister's house, the day of the arson incident. He also did not see her, nor did he call for her between. Instead, every week on his scheduled parenting time, he would send a text message asking for his visit and each time, I refused and replied to him with a simple "no." There was no fight from him, and he was not going to the school to visit her or anything, which carried on for roughly two months. Finally, on July 13, 2013, I received a minute order from the court stating: "The court has received numerous motions for contempt citation from father asserting that mother is not complying with current court orders regarding parenting time. The matter is being reviewed on 8/1/2013, and a GAL (Guardian Ad Litem) has been appointed. The court will advise the mother regarding the contempt citations at the 8/1 hearing orders: Each party is advised that all prior orders remain in full force and effect, and they are to fully comply with current court orders between now and the next court hearing. Failure to comply may result in the court modifying imposition of sanctions including fine and jail."

Chapter 5
The Guardian Ad Litem

The judge assigned Guardian Ad Litem, Bonnie Saltzman, to our custody case. She was the court-appointed child representative paid by the city and the liaison between the judge, us, and the child. A guardian ad item's job includes collecting and relaying information about each parent to the judge. The information is trusted to be unbiased and provided in a way that will aid the judge in determining the children's best interests. This approach in court procedure is taken when an attorney does not represent one or both parents or if the court needs an additional third-party opinion in high-conflict cases.

Once I received the notice, I immediately tried contacting her by phone and left several emails and voice messages that went unreturned within a span of two weeks. It was not until I sent her an email advising that I would ask the court to reassign someone else that she finally responded. The day we met Bonnie, I observed how unorganized she appeared. Caucasian woman, short, hippie-looking, and chaotic. I was waiting for her to light up a cigarette at any moment. The only thing going on in my mind was how busy she must have been, and thinking my case would be open and shut for her as I was more than willing to cooperate with her. I hoped to shed light on my concerns with this man's sudden, deep interest in my

The Truth is a Lie

daughter when I moved on with my life.

I told her that he and his love interest in Virginia disrespected me as our child's mother, and now, the same thing is happening with his wife but on a whole new level. I also mentioned that when our child was with him, he returned her to me with six-quarter-sized bald spots in her head and nightmares, and nobody batted an eye about it. I also expressed how he was attempting to separate families and alienate me from our child because the shit he was doing didn't make any damn sense. He kept saying, "if you need money from me to help you with my daughter, send her to me." But what is one hundred and twenty-seven dollars, and why was he making it seem like it was about money for me? He was just trying to adopt my son, knowing I was married. Put two and two together!

As we discussed the issues between the Bitter Deceiver and me, she immediately made it known that she had already had conversations with him and his wife. I had been attempting to contact her for weeks after she was assigned and did not get a response until I threatened her reassignment, so to hear that was beyond me. She spoke with them first. The narrative was already created, and the foundation for how she would think of my husband and me was already set in her mind. Plus, I do not think she was too fond of my email. As I explained my concerns to her, she looked at me as if she had heard all this before, totally disinterested in what I was saying. There were several things wrong with this picture from the beginning. And now we insert an overworked, underpaid public servant with no cultural knowledge about the urban community? Some of us were learning how to use the system to fight against injustice and catching on to shit.

In 2019, nearly six years after my dealings with family court, a video surfaced on YouTube featuring an ex-judge who became a whistle-blower in the California family court system titled: "Former Family Court Judge Exposes Bias Against Protective Parents." This video showed a clip from Fox 11 in Los Angeles, California, discussing the family court system for a series they were airing called "Lost in the System." Former family court judge Deann Salcido stated in her own words, "It's a jungle, it's a circus, and there is no ringmaster. It's a million-dollar industry in which the average citizens' interest is lost." She claims that judges are trained to hold bias towards women who raise issues with domestic violence and the timing on which it is raised. An article on domesticviolence.org says that domestic abuse is underreported. In 2017, the United Nations reported more than 87,000 murdered domestic violence victims. They also describe that only 25% of victims report physical attacks and worse when it comes to rape. Other statements show that women would have already been attacked 35 times by the time they reported domestic violence. Why is that?

The Truth is a Lie

The answer is simple. Fear. Since Colorado bases its custody on the best interest of children, when issues are raised in domestic situations, especially when children are involved, the system runs a fine line in violating a parent's fundamental right and responsibility to make decisions concerning the care, custody, and control of their children and the courts risk the threat of lawsuits. Have you noticed that every time CPS is involved in a situation, most child abuse and neglect findings are inconclusive? How can judges and court-appointed representatives effectively determine when abuse occurs if they do not speak the same language? In high-conflict cases, CPS runs the extreme financial risk of lawsuits because the entire judicial system is built on not knowing what you know, but showing what you can prove. Domestic abuse victims, whether physical, mental, or emotional, do not report mostly out of fear of retaliation, being demonized, and the mental conditioning that no matter where they run or how loud they scream, nobody will hear them. So why is the timing of domestic violence even a factor?

Although I had no prior knowledge of this and the particulars that went into the judge's school, I felt and understood what was going on but was unsure how to fight it. Bonnie advised me to follow the judge's order despite my concerns, fear of going to jail, and my child being in the wrong hands. I told her that I would. Right after court, I sent my child to be with them, but they decided to keep the charade going to get a rise out of me. They both did things to trigger me to make me look crazy and unfit. On May 30, 2013, I called my child's dentist because she needed a spacer and a couple of caps on her molars. When the receptionist discussed her care with me, she stopped and said, "Wait, didn't I talk to you about this yesterday?" I told her, "No, we never spoke." She said, "I remember speaking with you yesterday, and we went over payment and aftercare instructions." Again, she had me all the way confused, so I had her put our conversation in writing via email.

The email read: "On May 22, 2013, I received a series of calls from a woman regarding our patient. With all the many calls I receive each day and the amount of time that has passed, I could never say what her exact words were, but I was led to believe I was speaking to our patient's mom. She told me that the patient was in pain and had a possible tooth abscess. I told "mom" that her appointment with us in April had been referred to a pedodontist due to her age and needs. I remembered that our patient had come into the office for her first visit with her "dad" (my husband), so I thought it was possible that she had not gotten that information. Therefore, I gave "mom" the name and phone number of the pedodontist, Dr. Lucinda Lewis, and told her that Dr. Lewis would be the best provider to deal with in our patient's emergency.

In a span of five months, my daughter was taken from school, my truck was vandalized, we relocated where arson was done on my property, a child abuse allegation was made against me, my ex's wife was impersonating me, collecting my child's medical records, and a pending contempt of court hearing against me scheduled on August 1, 2013. These things were brought to Bonnie's attention, and nothing was investigated. Make it make sense! It completely amazes me that someone can come and disrupt our lives with no repercussions. Getting CPS involved would have been completely pointless as it seems none of them are properly trained for mental abuse.

I filed a motion to relocate to California for work purposes, I believe, in August. My husband had some upcoming dealings with a local television station to get his drum show aired as a series, and my job had new openings available in Los Angeles with better pay. It was a great idea for us to be able to seize the opportunity. During the Bitter Deceiver's parenting time, they both raised complaints about her having nightmares again, peeing in the bed, and that they were placing her in therapy without my consent or knowledge of the therapist. They would not provide me with any information concerning her mental health care. Every time my baby came home, I noticed her behavior changes. She was very reserved and quiet and wasn't her bubbly self anymore. I asked her about therapy, and she said she wasn't seeing anyone. To make issues even weirder, she told us she would see a shadow with red eyes in their house at night. Because of our Christian beliefs at the time, the only solution we could provide was to tell her to pray. Then we went to Dollar Tree and purchased a few little angels to protect her from whatever she said was scaring her. Other than that, and regardless of what she was saying, the only thing we knew to do, was document and monitor the situation.

Chapter 6
Maternal Instincts

One afternoon, I was sitting at my desk at work and received an email from Kristen about my daughter's behavior; at this point, I was sick of it. Why are they so adamant about finding issues with my child? When she was with us, she wasn't experiencing nightmares, bedwetting, or shadows with red eyes creeping her out. In fact, we spent the entire 2012 reassuring her from abandonment issues. Right after her email, I took an inventory of her personal information and immediately noticed that on every police report that was filed, she was listed under a different date of birth. She was recorded under three different birth years and months, but they weren't too far off. She also gave the courts false military service orders as a registered command officer stationed at the Buckley Air force Base.

I immediately went to Facebook and clicked on the Bitter Deceiver's page to see if I could find any clues about his wife since she had me blocked. As I was scrolling, I stumbled across a post from January where he announced what he was doing for her birthday. I compared the date of his post against the documents I had containing the data from the police reports and narrowed down her birthday to about January 11, 1983.

With this information, I searched her name and location and contrived with the date of birth. I wasn't making any progress. I had been trying to find out who she was for months before this. Frustrated and stressed, my desperate attempt to figure this out carried on for a couple of days between work breaks. Before long, I came up with the bright idea to search the Bitter Deceiver, and when I hit the "send" button, his mother, sister, and wife with the name listed Kristen Rose Pearson came up. Adrenaline surged through my body, causing me a high state of anxiety. I toggled back to the search engine, using the last name Pearson and there she was.

While my daughter was exercising her visits with her father and his family, I made sure to be extremely careful with my choice of words them. I was cooperative but stood my ground, and I was undeniably reasonable to make sure not to trigger this bitch to cause physical harm to my child. Since my concern was my child being emotionally manipulated by her stepmother, and her father not doing shit about it, I discontinued visitation against the judge's orders when they sent her back to me. The consequence of going to jail was the farthest from my mind. Since the motion to relocate was filed, the contempt of court hearing was rescheduled for September 19, 2013. At the hearing, despite everything I complained about, including the discoveries of the different birthdays when they asked me if I was afraid for my child's safety with her father, I told them I was concerned about his wife with my child when he was not home. I advised them of the safety concerns between them and my family because I believed they were attempting to get rid of us. They told me those concerns were not relevant to the current case and that I needed to take those issues up in criminal court. So now what? Bonnie didn't mention any of my concerns to the court or that she was looking into it. Bonnie gas lighted me as she made me believe these suspicious behaviors were acceptable, and although I'm bringing concerns to the court's attention, I could be accused of attempting to come in between the parent and child relationship, which is one of the "best interest" factors. I was still held in contempt of court, requested to pay a twenty-five dollar fine, and given strict demands by the judge to stop going against the judge's orders, or my punishment would be much worse.

The guardian ad litem is supposed to advocate for children. She wasn't representing me, but I trusted she would look deeper into my claims. This way, it could be reported accurately in court, and we could move on with our lives. Instead, I was looked at as this paranoid, bitter ex jealous of the new wife due to her negligence and lack of reporting.

Proceeding with the judge's orders once again and leaving it in God's hands, I was back to square one with all this mess. The guardian ad litem wasn't doing her job, and the courts were not listening to me. An attorney represented neither one of us. Bonnie requested information about my job and relocation, and I sent it to her like everything else. At the hearing, she said she never got it. Shortly after the hearing, I received an off-record minute order dated September 9, 2013, stating, "there is no time to further address a motion to relocate on the contempt of court hearing if it is a contested issue. It does not appear that a copy of the motion was sent to the (GAL), Bonnie Saltzman." The court date set for relocating was scheduled in November. I was given a deadline to accept the position. Unfortunately, I missed the opportunity because I wanted to ensure I could take my baby with me.

My daughter's visit with her father was approaching, and I could feel anxiety creeping in. I just knew as soon as she left, here we go with the bullshit again, and I refused to allow them to make me out to be "the crazy one." We were made aware Kristen was now pregnant with twins. My daughter would express how Kristen treated her differently than her biological children, especially when her father was not home and forcing her to call her "mom." Of course, we all knew this entire ordeal was a front from the beginning. None of this was out of real care and concern for my child. To them, this was a huge game to see who the courts would say the better parent was, and they were going to do anything to turn this conspiracy into a truth.

My baby gets to her father's house, and I brace myself for emotional impact. As I suspected, Kristen sent me an email on October 7, 2013, saying: "Hey, I got a call from nutritional services about a balance. I believe the 'Bitter Deceiver' mentioned it to you, and I don't know if you guys took care of it or not. I was wondering so I know to disregard or not." I replied: "You can disregard it. It was taken care of last week." They shouldn't be calling anymore." I also stated, "I don't know if you and the Bitter Deceiver are communicating about our daughter, but I sent her a navy and light blue uniform shirt that I believe is at your house. She was almost sent home on Friday due to her not having her shirt when you sent her to school. I'm sending you to say I don't care if her uniforms are dirty. Please send them back." They would intentionally keep her uniforms and articles of her clothing and not send them back. Kristen would claim that the shirts at her home belonged to her children as they wore the same uniform colors.

Although I found this to be exceptionally annoying and inconvenient, I kept my cool cause now; I'm getting ready to fuck with her head a little bit. First, she reached out to me to pick up a written altercation. I knew exactly what she was doing. She kept going on about why I didn't like her and finally revealed that I knew she was a fraud. I said: "This matter has nothing to do with why I don't like you. Or me and you, for that matter. This pertains to the facts about me and the Bitter Deceiver parenting our child. His motive to move was to not be child supported and try to prove how much he's been there for our child, which he can't. The reason for the spray paint on my truck was that I didn't make it to court and the case be dismissed. The motive for the arson was trying to get rid of me so he could be in place to have her. Same with contempt. I'm not doing anything to either of you, but you always try to find fault. What was the point of moving to Colorado being secretive? What's with all the secrets? I don't know if you believe in astrology, but I'm a Capricorn. And so are you. I know things about you that you don't think I know. Because just our cardinal signs, we find out, and we're not to be played with. I pulled an SCRA on you the other day, and it shows you're still active military Army status since, I think, 2006. I know your maiden name and date of birth, and that's all I will tell you. But you and me? There's no relevance to the situation. All I care about is that my child is safe and okay." She said I might have had her date of birth correct, but everything else was incorrect. She then called me a stalker and a bad one at that. The bickering went on in a few rounds of emails until I finally revealed her last name to her. She flips out, tries to probe me for information, and threatens to tell my job I was misusing company time and resources.

Two days later, I got a call from human resources. They asked me about the ordeal between Kristen and me because she called to file a complaint against me. I told them I went to the Service members Civil Relief Act (SCRA) website, which is accessible to the public, to find out her military status. It wasn't done on company time, but I did use the company computer to search for the break-in information, so there was that. Due to the severity of the complaint, I was given a verbal warning and sent back to work. The next day, I was served with a restraining order for stalking and harassment. The date for that was scheduled for October 24, 2013.

On October 10, 2013, I emailed Bonnie and said: "Hi Bonnie, I'm reaching out to you because I haven't heard from anyone and was hoping you were affected by this "Government Shutdown" stuff that's happening. According to the "Bitter Deceiver's" wife, Kristen, our daughter has been taking things from their house and lying to them. She advised that my child may need to see a doctor. At our court hearing on 9/19/2013, the "Bitter Deceiver" stated that he has a family therapist involved, but when I asked my child if anyone had reached out to talk to her or if she was getting any help, she said 'no.' My daughter told me yesterday that her stepmother spanked her the other day, but I wasn't sure why. Now, if they are seeing a therapist, I believe they would provide alternatives for disciplining a child. I tried to get an attorney to represent me for the remainder of the case, but the legal services I was seeking, sent me to a legal clinic, and they can't represent a case already in process. My daughter is going through enough, and all I can do is try to make it easy for her, but I'm starting to feel like no one cares or has the time to sit down and see exactly what's going on. Is there anything I need to do before we return to court on 11/14? Will you still be visiting with my daughter or her father and me? There is a twist to this situation. Kristen Pearson, Joseph's wife, is still active military. I found out through a public website. She hasn't been working, nor is she near an army base. You can't google her; you can't locate her on the white pages. Although she's not relevant to our custody case, she does provide care for my child for the majority of the time. If she's AWOL right now, it will make sense why they both are being so secretive about their whereabouts and lying to Judge Ashby about where they live. It took me since April to find her maiden name and date of birth. I just wanted to let you know in case you need it in the future.

Bonnie replies, "I have not gone anywhere. I met with the Bitter Deceiver and his wife. I will be going to the school to see your daughter. I will investigate the concerns outlined in your email. I do know that Buckley Air Force Base is a multi-agency facility. I have worked with other army and navy personnel based there." She also asked me to print and send me everything I had in writing. I have a record of what she requested, and the receipt that the documents weighed 1.20 lbs. cost me time and $7.89 to send to her via FedEx. I might as well have thrown it in the trash after none of this was investigated. I also noticed that she had more dealings with the Bitter Deceiver and his wife than she did with me, and I was the one who was primarily physically responsible for my child, according to the order. I was also the one pleading for help for my daughter.

On October 16, 2013, around 6 pm, about a day after sending my daughter back to be with her father, I received a call from an

The Truth is a Lie

unidentified number. Usually, I wouldn't answer, but I decided to entertain the call. When I picked up, Kristen said, "you're dealing with the baddest bitch of all time, and when this is over, I'm going to kill you." Lawd have mercy, really? Who says that? I called the Aurora Police, and when they showed up, I told them everything that had happened up to this point. I provided them with her last name and the address on record with the court.

I invited the officers to my home. We sat down and talked a little more about the situation, and the officer said this is all strange because our records show Kristen Smith registered for a driver's license at the address you provided me earlier today. Then he pulled out his laptop, turned it towards me, and asked, "Is this her?" When I looked at the picture, it was a photo of a Caucasian woman with blonde hair and blue eyes. I said "no" the description I provided over the phone was an African American woman. Now, we were all confused. The officer proceeded to tell me that they were working up an investigation on Kristen. Allegedly, she has been out of the military for over one year, and Texas police officers placed a warrant for her arrest. Allegedly, there were two warrants out for her arrest in Texas. One of them was extraditable, and the other one was not. Bonnie said since she was not arrested on a Texas warrant when they went to her home, there was no Texas warrant at that time, and once again, she did not investigate it. I sent Bonnie an email advising her of what transpired the day after, and she responded to me, saying, "I wish you would have told me about the threats yesterday." At this point, I was done with her ass.

October 24th. The day of the restraining order was wild. When I got there, Kristen sat to the right of me, her eyes fixed on the judge. She didn't look my way, not even with her peripheral vision. You could see her attempt to block me out. I know she already thought she won with that ugly smirk on her face. The Bitter Deceiver was standing in the back of the courtroom, looking like he hadn't slept in days! Kristen also did not appear to be pregnant. She should have appeared to be about eight months pregnant at this time. When we were aware of her pregnancy, she was "already" a few months along. She had no belly bump whatsoever on this day.

The courts allowed her to speak about why she needed a restraining order at the hearing. Her voice was small and shaking. Not loud and confident like any other time. She couldn't come up with a real reason why she feared her life was in jeopardy by little old me. Now, it was time for me to speak... I pulled out a wad of papers that contained all the documents I sent to the guardian ad litem, plus an unclassified response to my email from the U.S. Army's crime tips alias stating they located her name under Smith, but she is no longer with the US Army. She finally glanced at me with a side eye, and I noticed her hands started shaking even harder. She was unaware of the documents I had. She assumed that I thought she was still in the military and was dying to know what I knew

The Truth is a Lie

about her. Let's see how bad of a stalker I am now.

When it was my turn to speak, I placed all the papers in front of me and eloquently spoke to the judge, matter of fact, without emotion. I informed him of the issues we were facing and that everything we were going through was unnecessary but highly concerning. I looked to my right and stared at Kristen for a short moment. I felt my anger building. The pressure in my body felt slow and thick, and my heart was pumping through my chest as I held myself back from jumping across and risking it all. The tension in the air was so heavy; it was like a bunch of elephants took several seats. The judge ordered me not to look at the plaintiff as she fixed her eyes on him. I calmly looked back at him and stated: "I have a stack of dates of birth and different aliases for Kristen that she provided to public officials, but if we compare the information we have on these documents and the date that was put on this restraining order; which now she used my daughter's date of birth and her birth year, who exactly will you be protecting, your Honor?" the judge annoyingly asked to see the papers, yelled at the both of us and said, "This is not Jerry Springer, and a child's life is at stake. You're both going to grow up and figure this out!" I understand why the judge scolded both of us, as he had to be impartial to the issue. He then asked for the documents for his records and terminated her complaint of harassment and stalking against me.

INDY GOHARD

When the judge dismissed us from the courtroom, Kristen and the Bitter Deceiver were both standing in the hallway with the look of disappointment and defeat on their faces. I also saw an officer waiting at the door, but I didn't think anything of it. I quickly left the building and returned to work. It was a couple of days before I saw my baby girl as she was visiting with her father. He would never allow telephone communications between us when she was at his home. This was something I also bought to Bonnie's attention but was told I didn't need to speak with her when she was exercising her visits with her extended family. Not even to check on her.

As you can imagine, I could hardly wait for my baby girl to come home. When her father returned her, she told me that her stepmom was not at home that entire weekend. I found out months later that Arapahoe county courts placed her in jail for that same outstanding warrant out of Texas that Bonnie said didn't exist. When I told Bonnie the judge dismissed the restraining order, she never followed up on that either. So far, this woman has done a fantastic job at doing absolutely nothing regarding the important matters concerning my child's wellbeing.

The relocation hearing was scheduled in November, which came and went. Again, Bonnie never followed up with my HR to confirm anything, the deadline for me to accept the job offer was missed, and my husband's TV pilot wasn't set in stone, so there was no longer a need to move at that time. Thanksgiving and Christmas were a breeze as we split the holidays. Of course, they were a little messy, but not unbearable. The final custody hearing was scheduled for January 2014.

Before the hearing, I sent the Bitter Deceiver an email attempting to arrange our daughter's 8th birthday because she wanted her step-siblings to attend. Now you know they had an issue with that. They weren't interested in anything that looked like co-parenting or co-existing. Are you silly? You couldn't possibly think they would be willing to call a truce after all the fucked-up shit they did to my family and me, could you? My willingness to be the bigger person was my demonstration to place my child's needs above my own because I should have been in jail the first time she laid her hands on my child. As God was my witness, the only thing that kept me was my faith in God and knowing that there was a bigger reason for all this.

I had moments of extreme doubt, crying, sobbing at night, and asking why I was going through this nightmare. I lost my grandmother the year before and still hadn't grieved her loss, so going through this right after having a baby was psychologically taxing on me. I remember being on my knees, crying to God and being angry at myself for putting myself and my children in this position. There were things I could control and couldn't, which was hard for me to accept. At this moment, I received a huge amount of support from my husband, which was refreshing because the year before our marriage was rocky, we were already on the verge of being over, and we didn't even break one year of matrimony when divorce was threatened. I took a mental note of this and was more concerned with the mental state of my daughter, knowing these people didn't give a shit. To them, she is just case number 2012JV1234.

At the final custody hearing, Bonnie never addressed any of the issues or concerns I laid before her. Not even the recent issue we had with him not seeking medical care for her when her retainer broke in her mouth and dug into her inner right cheek. He took her to school, and she was in pain and injured all day. He never told me about it. This was something else I bought to Bonnie that went unaddressed. The warrant was never mentioned. She discussed a little about the restraining order and that it was dropped. She made it seem like we were this big happy family who needed to learn to trust each other. If this is how you all think and move in high-conflict cases, you are way behind, and continuing to do things this way, will not move the needle forward and will continue to put families in danger. Neither one of us was allowed to speak at this hearing. After listening to the case, assuming everything was going well, no issues had arisen since November, and the Bitter Deceiver exercised his parenting time as scheduled, the judge decided to split our visitation and

The Truth is a Lie

decision-making down the middle. Wait, what?!?!?

I stood up, heartbroken. Not because I lost. But because I understood I had a long road with these fucking fools. I was angry, and I questioned my sanity. I questioned if I did everything correctly, how this mess would end as I was the only one willing to let bygones be bygones for the sake of my baby's happiness, and I was fucking tired! I quietly said to myself, "Lord, why?" but held myself together and didn't break emotion. Not in front of them.

When I stood up, I turned around, and I saw the Bitter Deceiver's mother and wife sitting in the audience, and they appeared happy about the decision. When Kristen stood up, I noticed her belly was huge. It made no sense to me because I just saw her three months before in court for the restraining order, and there was no way she could have been that far along. I remember wondering if her belly was fake because when she turned around towards the back, you could see the straps and tell they weren't from a bra. But none of that had anything to do with me. If I had known then, what I know now, I would have filed a complaint against Bonnie's oversight and lack of reporting and an appeal. She took advantage of my ignorance of the law and violated my fundamental right and responsibility to make decisions concerning the care, custody, and control of my child's safety and well-being. When I got home that evening, I cried so loud on the side of my bed, asking God what to do and feeling completely helpless because I knew in my heart that Bonnie's recommendation to the court was not in the best interest of my child. I will explain why later, but let's get to what happens next.

Chapter 7
My Sister's Keeper

The evening after the final custody hearing was tough. Kristen was "supposedly" getting ready to have her twins very soon, and everything was quiet, but my spirit was so bothered. Three weeks later, during my daughter's visit with her father, I was overcome by the feeling of guilt and shame but couldn't figure out for the life of me where these feelings were coming from. Could it have been the fact that Mercury was getting ready to enter retrograde the next day? Was it that; I felt that I failed my daughter? My intuition told me something bad was happening in the cosmos, and I just didn't know what.

On February 5th and 6th, 2014, Denver temperatures were between negative 8- and 11- degrees mid-winter. I went on Facebook that evening with a heavy heart. I posted a prayer specifically for people in the cold, especially those with little children, and I left the rest in God's hands. Friday, February 7, 2014, was a normal workday at the job. Things were seemingly quiet, and I had a little hope that we could all be cordial and work this parenting agreement out. We still weren't talking, but no one was fighting either. On my first fifteen-minute break, I walked into the breakroom, logged on to Facebook like usual, and scrolled passed a news article that said, "Missing 5-Day Old Baby." I was interested in reading the story, but my break was getting ready to end, so I hurried back to my desk and got back to work. I didn't think to log back online for the rest of my time at work. As I was driving home, the Bitter Deceiver's aunt called me in a state of shock. She said, "did you hear about that crazy wife of the Bitter Deceiver?" I told her 'No,' and she goes, "she kidnapped a baby!"

    Immediately I remembered the article from earlier, and when I pulled into the driveway, I ended the call with his aunt and went straight to my phone to Google the article. The story hit major media outlets on the home screen and was a top story already. The first thing I saw was a bold tile from People.com and her mugshot from Cedar County, Iowa, that said, "Kristen Smith Arrested in the Kidnapping of Kayden Powell." "A woman who pretended to be pregnant stole her half-sister's newborn son and left him in a storage crate."

The Truth is a Lie

Photo: Cedar County Sheriff's Office

My eyes welled with tears, and I sat in my freezing car for five minutes, imagining what it would be like to be inside a freezing box in complete darkness. I looked down at my phone and continued to read.

An article from the Associated Press at People magazine sourced:

"An hour after a woman reported her newborn son missing from a Wisconsin home, police questioned her sister – found with a prosthetic pregnancy belly, baby clothes and a stroller, but no baby, according to court documents. It was more than 24 hours after Kayden Powell went missing before authorities discovered the infant, less than a week old, in a plastic storage crate outside an

Iowa gas station, miraculously alive and well despite frigid temperatures.

Kristen Smith of Denver had pretended to be pregnant, went to Wisconsin and stole her sister's baby from his bassinet as his parents slept, court documents say. Then, as police closed in on her, she allegedly abandoned the infant swaddled in blankets. Federal prosecutors in Madison charged Smith with kidnapping Friday afternoon, hours after an Iowa police chief found Kayden. He's strong," the newborn's great-uncle, Mark Bennett, said of the boy. "I'm glad baby is still living instead of in a ditch somewhere on a strange highway."

Missing Baby Mystery

The discovery of the infant shortly after 10 a.m. Friday caught a frantic search involving police officers in Wisconsin, Illinois and Iowa. It began after the boy's mother, Brianna Marshall, called the police around 4:30 a.m. Thursday to report her newborn had vanished from Bennett's home, where she and the baby's father, Bruce Powell, had been staying, according to police and the affidavit. Marshall said Smith had left the house a couple of hours earlier to return to Colorado. While police were at the house, Smith called on her cell phone. She told police that Marshall and Bruce Powell were planning to move to Denver on Saturday to live with her, and she had Kayden's clothes in her car but didn't have

The Truth is a Lie

the boy.

Police told her to pull over for questioning. An officer met her at a Kum & Go gas station near Interstate 80 in West Branch, Iowa. The affidavit says she was arrested about 5:30 a.m. on an outstanding Texas warrant, but she denied any knowledge of Kayden's whereabouts. A search of her cellphone revealed emails in which she said she gave birth on Feb. 5, according to the court document. A search of her Facebook page turned up postings in which she claimed she was pregnant. Smith didn't appear pregnant, according to the affidavit. A pregnancy test that was administered while she was in custody came back negative, U.S. Attorney John Vaudreuil said. A Miraculous Discovery

Meanwhile, dozens of officers began searching for the child at possible stop-offs along Smith's route from Wisconsin to Iowa. West Branch Police Chief Mike Horihan decided to check the area around a BP station about 500 yards from the station where Smith was arrested.

He heard a baby's cries and discovered Kayden in a closed storage crate alongside the building. The newborn was responsive and healthy, the chief said. "I had tears in my eyes," BP station manager Jay Patel said, recalling his reaction to the police chief telling him that the infant had been found. "It's good news, but it's sad, too." Temperatures in West Branch, about 180 miles southwest of the Town of Beloit, dipped below zero Thursday night into Friday. They were still in the single digits when the baby was found. "Surprisingly, with the weather the way it was, he was surprisingly healthy," said Horihan, the Iowa police chief. "To be honest with you, that's not what I expected." The baby was taken to an Iowa City hospital, where he was reunited with his parents and released Friday evening.

Online court records didn't list a defense attorney for Smith. She faces life in prison if convicted. Police interviewed Smith again after Kayden was discovered, the affidavit said. She admitted she had taken the baby and left him at the BP station. Bennett, the baby's great-uncle, told The Associated Press he first met Smith on Thursday night, when he came home and found her, his mother and the baby's mother and father in his house. He said his mother later explained that Marshall and her sister had the same father but different mothers. He went to his room in the basement. When he woke up, the baby and Smith were gone. He said he kept telling Marshall that Smith had to have taken the child, but Marshall refused to believe it. The baby's bassinet was two feet from the parent's bed, and he found a paring knife on the ground next to it.

"I could have woken up to a bloody mess," Bennett said.

He said he hopes Smith gets locked up for life.

The Truth is a Lie

"You stole him like you're stealing something from the grocery store," the great-uncle said. *"Nobody in their right mind should have thought of that."*

The part in the article that blew me away was this:

"Checkered Past

Authorities said that Smith appears to go by multiple names and has had run-ins with the law in multiple states. The Texas warrant stems from a felony indictment charging her with tampering with government documents late last year while she was in jail in Colorado. A spokesman for the Arapahoe County, Colo., sheriff's office declined to discuss the details of her arrest there. A spokeswoman for the district attorney's office in Tarrant County, Texas, said it's not clear why Colorado authorities released Smith instead of sending her back to Texas."

Isn't this the same warrant I told Bonnie about back in October? It wasn't until I read this article that I learned Kristen went to jail right after our hearing for the restraining order in November. The same hearing, she wasn't pregnant. Why didn't Bonnie know that Kristen went to jail that day, and why didn't she follow up on the Texas warrant? My daughter's grandmother dropped her off the following day. When she came home, she was unaware of what had happened. I asked her where her stepmother was, and she told me that she had fallen down the stairs around Wednesday night and gone to the hospital alone. Before my daughter returned, I immediately took my issue with Colorado courts to the media. My interview was about my warning to the public about the court system. Not Kristen. After the media edited the footage, the story they conveyed to the public was Kristen was harassing me. The two Colorado media outlets that took my interview ultimately removed them from their archives and YouTube, but I was able to locate a clip taken from an Iowa news station which kind of shows what I was talking about.

Photo: Associated Press Iowa CBS 2/FOX 28

I took the relocation money we saved and hired an attorney to file an emergency hearing. After the interviews, the FBI contacted and interviewed my husband and me, and we told them the actions of Kristen and the Bitter Deceiver leading up to this baby's kidnapping. Remember, she kidnapped my baby first. I also found out from other media sources that Kristen gave her sister and her boyfriend sleeping medication before taking their baby. I immediately thought about the brownie my daughter ate when she kidnapped her. When I arrived at court, Bonnie was there. Still looking dusty as ever and standing next to the Bitter Deceiver.

She swiftly walked up to me, I smiled at her and said, "hi." But she was furious. She gets in my face and whispers loudly, "I was mortified when I saw you on the news!" while pointing at herself. 'Tuh! Was I supposed to feel bad?" Funny how she wasn't mortified that a four-day-old was found alive inside a crate in freezing temperatures and survived for thirty hours! I didn't last twenty minutes in my car. None of this would have happened if she had done her fucking job! My attorney didn't help either because with Kristen now in jail, the threat of her harming my child was gone, but what about the Bitter Deceiver? Did he not know his wife wasn't pregnant? Is he responsible enough to make sound decisions concerning our child? Do these things matter?

There was no evidence that he was under investigation from the FBI except officers saying they were investigating him, but nothing in writing. I trusted my attorney to do what was needed to reverse the judge's decision. Once again, I was let down. What the hell is really going on here? I even had a screenshot of a Facebook post with him telling Kristen's sister that she was trying to help them. None of that mattered. The court's systems are seemingly worse than the people we come to protect ourselves and our children from! Bonnie never apologized to me for this oversight or her misconduct. And to this day, I still feel the Bitter Deceiver knows more about this situation than he's willing to discuss because what were they going to do with the baby?

Chapter 8
A Long Road Ahead

The beginning of the year apparently threw us all for a loop. Nothing made sense. I felt like we were all in this twilight zone. Despite all the lectures and oversight, the fact that justice was not served in my daughter's case made me look at the justice system totally differently than what I was blessed to experience while in kinship care with my grandmother. My case managers listened to me when I needed guidance. They provided resources, even family therapy, to my family and me, and they followed up with us on schedule.

Shout out to my grandmother, who was willing to accept the help offered. And big ups to Jack Jackson and John Beltz, former City and County of Denver case managers. If you are still alive and read this, you both were a fundamental part of who I have become and my desire to advocate for children. Experiencing this gave me a deeper sense of purpose, but now I must learn to move on with peace and grace, knowing that nobody would be held accountable for what just happened. We're supposed to just move on and act like that never happened. Hmm…. Just doesn't sit well in my spirit.

Today, I turn on the news and see people losing their lives in cases where suspicions were placed on the wrong person and victims are being villainized in high conflict or divorce cases. These situations typically end with a person either being murdered or missing. Remember Christopher Watts? The Colorado man who annihilated his entire family because he was living a double life decided that killing his baby girls and pregnant wife was the best decision for him. I could relate to something leading to a similar setting which was again overlooked by different Colorado jurisdiction.

With all the chaos, pending court dates for Kristen, and the new visitation schedule, I still showed compassion toward the Bitter Deceiver giving him the benefit of the doubt of his knowledge or lack thereof, of his wife's pregnancy. The FBI genuinely believed; he did not know. There was nothing else I could do but continue the visitation as ordered. In August of that year, my father had a major stroke. Our daughter was eight years old and desired to spend more time with her father. Assuming he was the responsible adult he fought to prove in the courts that he was, we agreed she would finish elementary with us, and when middle school started, she could go to a school closer to him as he claimed he desired more time with her as well. That was my wiliness to continue establishing a parent-child relationship outside of Bonnie's recommendation, as co-parenting seemed to be going well. I still had my doubts, but I was optimistic. I wanted this for her.

I left the company I was working for as a foreclosure specialist that summer to focus on helping juveniles in the justice

The Truth is a Lie

system with my non-profit called Building Achievers for Life Network Inc. It was a recidivism program created to help young men between the age of 12 and 19 find their purpose. I developed a business plan, partnered with the City and County of Aurora and the church we were members of, and came up with creative, fun, and economically driven ways for them to carry out their community service sentence. For about six months after I left my job, I served the church and used my 401k to pay the bills for the remainder of the year. This gave me a break to do what I wanted to while also having the time to focus on my father, who just became ill.

After my father's stroke, my husband and I started having problems again. Once he completed the treatment program in 2011, he returned to drinking. He was still battling this addiction; it was kicking his ass. There were moments when he would stop drinking for months, do a great job, and stay out of trouble, but that's when he wasn't accepting drumming gigs outside of the church. For three years, I would beg him to seek additional help, but he never thought he had a problem. I alerted his parents, particularly his mother, and she would excuse his behavior or try to find a reason for me being the problem. But I said what I said, and at least it wasn't a secret.

The entire year 2014 was exceptionally tough. My father was moved to a rehabilitation facility sometime in November or December. My husband and I were going through it badly. His life was very complicated, and somehow, he made his schedule and gigs more important than the needs of our family most times. Thinking back, we didn't spend a lot of time building together. The prior year we were battling this custody case, and the year before, I was dealing with the loss of my grandmother, so I wasn't paying attention to what he was doing while I was mentally battling all this. I knew that whatever I was going through didn't help him either.

Chapter 9
The Manipulative Deceiver

Being that I was in the Christian faith with him, I took my vows seriously and was willing to go through this storm with him for better or worse, in sickness and health. I figured if we keep God in the midst of everything, we will be okay. I continued to attend church every Sunday or at whatever church he played. He also began accepting club gigs again.

It was either during Thanksgiving or right before Christmas 2014 when my father was moved to the new rehab center from the hospital. About a week into his getting there, I received a call from the director of the program threatening to discontinue our visits with my father because, unbeknown to me, my husband decided it would be a great idea to show up to the place, under the influence, entering the patient's rooms, and recording them to declare negligence on the workers. I was so embarrassed. He got upset that I was mad at him, and we argued about the situation. My issue was that he never thought anything he did was wrong and justified everything he did. No one held him accountable but me, and anyone who tried, made it to his shit list fast. But I could give two shits about this list.

About a week after this incident, I go back to the facility to visit my dad, and my husband went to pick up my son and oldest daughter from my brother's house. Before he left, we argued again about the situation and just him, needing to get help. I got out of the car, and he quickly drove away. It was dark. I didn't have a ride home, and it was freezing. I started walking towards my brother's house and praying to God, asking him for a sign. Between the courts, our families, and my husband making me question my beliefs on things I was passionate about and trying to keep my identity in all this, I pacified the conflict by going with "whatever" to keep the peace and I was just done doing it anymore. He knew how I felt about him drinking and driving. After he left my brother's house, I couldn't get in contact with him. Shortly after a few failed attempts, I called my brother. He came, picked me up, and took me home.

When I got home, my son said the Manipulative Deceiver (my husband) was in the garage and was hurt. He said he believed he heard him fall. I didn't pay any attention to him because I felt like that was exactly what he wanted from me. Before long, he comes into the house on the verge of tears and holding his left shoulder. He said he was coming down the stairs after leaving my brother's house, and on his way down, he slipped and fell forward, hitting his shoulder on the icy concrete steps. The man fucked himself up. I felt bad for him; worst of all, he did not have health insurance.

Literally, three days after this incident, he was driving, and I was in the passenger seat. It was snowing, and a woman to the left was attempting to stop but slid past the stop sign causing us to bump into her. The Manipulative Deceiver contacted our family attorney,

The Truth is a Lie

and they began the process of finding the other driver at fault.

I'm getting ready to turn 30 and find out I'm pregnant with my fourth child, our second child together. We looked at it as a brand-new start. Nobody outside our families but a couple of my good friends knew what we were going through in our relationship. Despite it all, they were all in support of us keeping our family together. I didn't go on social media to put our business out there or shame our relationship in any way. As far as anyone else knew, including our church family, as long as we posted positivity, we had a beautiful, blended family. One of many things I didn't like was our moral support was separate. I had people who had my back, and he had folks that had his. With his charm and innocent demeanor, he is skilled at getting people to like to him, but behind closed doors and that bottle, he is a monster.

My father was discharged from the facility and released into my care. The Manipulative Deceiver started treating me exceptionally well during this pregnancy, and from the looks of it, his drinking was under control. He was still drinking, but he wasn't getting belligerent and once again, just like he was behaving when the Bitter Deceiver was around, he was on his best behavior. I thought it was so weird how he could turn on and off when he wanted to especially when others were around, and I began thinking his issues were deeper than I thought. The entire time my father was there, we had very little problems.

INDY GOHARD

In February 2015, when our living situation with my dad began to normalize, I found employment at another loan servicing place. The money I had ran out, and I needed to get back to supporting my family. The jobs the Manipulative Deceiver had never sustained our family. His money was enough to take care of himself and our few bills, and I paid the rent and everything else we needed to keep the house afloat. Six months later, the company downsized and terminated my position while on maternity leave. The company offered me severance pay, and I was able to collect unemployment and stay home with my baby comfortably until the following year. It was approaching one year my dad would be living with us. He was rehabilitated in my home, where the Manipulative Deceiver took over his care once I returned to work. Although he has injured himself, I must give him credit for looking after my pops. Two months after I started working, my dad returned home once his in-home care was approved.

April 2015, The Manipulative Deceiver was scheduled for shoulder surgery at the same time my dad returned home. When I got to the hospital to pick him up, he was coming out of his sedation from being under general anesthesia. The doctors advised that he didn't do anything strenuous and rest for the next twenty-four hours following the surgery. When we arrived home, we were greeted by his little brother, who was staying with us at the time. My son was with his father, and my oldest daughter was with hers. We had our

The Truth is a Lie

daughter, and I was almost 17 weeks pregnant.

We get home, and I start preparing dinner. Chicken and waffles were on the menu. I get him in the bed, run upstairs, and grab my grandmother's old rice pot, which had one handle hanging on for dear life. This was my favorite pot to deep fry chicken in. It just did what it was supposed to do and gave what it was supposed to give. I put the grease in the pot, rinsed and seasoned my chicken, and took out the little bit of flour I had left to batter the chicken. I had just enough to coat the few pieces I was getting ready to fry. I ran downstairs, thinking I would check on the Manipulative Deceiver and then I called my dad to pass the time for the grease to heat up. At what seemed to be about six minutes in, I hear the Manipulative Deceiver's brother yelling, attempting to get our attention. I told my dad I would call him back, and when I walked to the bottom of the stairs, I noticed thick black smoke above my brother-in-law's head, and he yelled out, "there's a fire in here!" I ran upstairs. As we headed up towards the kitchen, the house was dark, and the smoke had to be about twelve inches thick.

The smoke detectors were going off upstairs, but we didn't hear them until we ran out of the room. All I could see were the flames coming from the kitchen as we got to the top of the stairs. The Manipulative Deceiver was behind me, and we ran to the kitchen. My brother-in-law grabbed our daughter and ran outside. The Manipulative Deceiver and I stood in front of the fire for about two seconds, trying to figure out what to do. We had no fire extinguisher, and the flour and salt were not enough to put these flames out.

I had to think fast. I quickly turned the stove off and moved the can of old grease that was next to the flames out of the way. Per his doctor's orders, the Manipulative Deceiver was not supposed to be doing anything but resting. I don't know if this reaction was part of the anesthesia, but he stared at the flames, and his eyes grew in amazement like he just saw the most beautiful work of art in life, all while I frantically looked around the kitchen to find oven mitts. Then I remembered there was only one handle on the pot, which was not stable! I looked up to see the flames melting the range hood through the thick smoke, and now my lungs were starting to burn like inhaling ground cayenne pepper. I run to the cabinets looking for oven mitts with no luck. As I arose, I saw a gardening glove on the counter next to the sink. It was the thick ones with cloth material on the outside. Without thinking or putting it on my hand, I balled it in the center of my hand and grabbed the handle of the flaming pot.

Once I had a good hold, out of instinct, my other hand gripped my wrist to stabilize the handle, and when I looked up, the Manipulative Deceiver was headed towards the back door to open it. He opened the door, and a bellow of smoke followed the direction of the wind outside. He ran outside, stood behind the door, and held it open for me.

The Truth is a Lie

With my arms completely extended out and my hand still clinching my wrist, I slowly walked towards the door with the pot of flames in my hands, trying not to tip it or have the flames burn my face or clothing. I approached the open door, and there were only two ways I could throw it, either forward out of the house or to the left down the stairs of our two-story home. The Manipulative Deceiver was holding and standing behind the door to my right. Then I hear him yell, "throw it down the stairs!"

As soon as my hands were out of the house, I quickly tossed the burning pot down the stairs. It was dark, and the backyard lights were off. When I let go, I heard the grease from the pot splash, a loud "dong" as the pot made contact with the concrete, and immediately I heard screaming. I panicked, thinking my brother-in-law ran to the backyard with my daughter when he ran outside with her. I flipped on the light switch, and when I looked down the stairs, the Manipulative Deceiver stripped himself naked from his clothes, screaming and running in circles. How the hell did his ass get down there? Why would he jump from behind the door where he was safe and down the stairs in the same direction he told me to throw the pot? To this day, I wonder, what if I had thrown it forward? He would have jumped right into the pot. Why?

The fire department gets to our house and takes a statement from his brother and us. I felt so bad. Everything happened so quickly. It must have taken about ten minutes from when we were notified about the fire until the fire department arrived. He literally just left one hospital and immediately headed to another under completely different circumstances. The fire department transports both of us to the hospital in different vehicles. I was carried by ambulance, and the fire department took him. We both arrived and entered the hospital at the same time.

He was in bad shape but still smiling. He repeatedly asked me if I was okay. I asked him if he was okay, too. We both said we loved each other and were wheeled into our rooms. Nurses conducted a quick fetal checkup and treated me for smoke inhalation with oxygen. I felt entirely better within minutes. After about an hour of monitoring, I was discharged from their care, and within minutes of my release, his family arrived from Colorado Springs to support us both. He spent seven days in the hospital being treated for his injured left shoulder, right leg, and feet, where he suffered second, and third-degree burns. While he was in the hospital, I carried on our daughter's third birthday party with close family. She was so happy, and I was grateful that all was not lost for any of us due to this freak accident.

In August 2015, our baby was born. Our baby boy wasn't nearly as dark or small as our first child. He was two and a half pounds heavier than his sister, with no pigment and slanted eyes. My baby favored my dad and me. Our daughter was the spitting image of her father. He would comment on him, calling him a "house

The Truth is a Lie

nigga" and I would catch him staring at him to look for similarities. He didn't look anything like his father, I must admit. But we all know even in homes where fidelity is never questioned, genetics are funny like that.

Six weeks after the baby boy was born, I got a call from human resources about my new job, and they told me they were downsizing and terminating my position. They offered me a severance pay of fifteen thousand dollars, and I collected unemployment. Although I felt like the rug was ripped from under me, I took this opportunity to be with my baby and focused on my non-profit, which was getting ready to go live at our church.

The Manipulative Deceiver was taking all kinds of gigs at this point. He was always gone. With all that was going on, I arranged for my oldest daughter to be with her father primarily. I went to child support enforcement and had them cease garnishments a few months before the arrangement. We were cordial and communicated like adults. And, of course, you know the Manipulative Deceiver had an issue with this, but he didn't see the bigger picture. I don't understand for the life of me why anyone would want to see ex-spouses fighting while children are involved. I took my vows seriously; no side communications were going on between him and me, and he was seemingly in a new, loving relationship with a baby on the way. I was happy for him. My daughter started expressing a desire to be with her father, so I sent her with him and saw her anytime I wanted to.

When I dropped her off at her father's home, unbeknown to me he would take her to his sister's home. (The one who really doesn't like me). This carried on through the following year. His sister's husband notified me of this arrangement when they began experiencing their own issues, but she was allowed to stay while I got things figured out with the Manipulative Deceiver, as her home was seemingly more stable than mine.

I felt resentment from the Manipulative Deceiver regarding the fire, but he would never admit it. Although he treated me well during our second pregnancy, something still felt off. He was always a very passive-aggressive man. He's the type of person who would talk you into doing something you wouldn't normally do and when your feet met the flame, he would ask, "whose problem is that?" If I weren't willing to give him a ride to work and back, he would get rides from women and sit in front of our house with them laughing and smoking just to get a rise out of me. One time, I went outside, walked over to the side he was sitting on, opened that lady's door and told his ass to get out. How dare either one of them think that was, okay? It was the utter disrespect that made everything so bad.

Later that year, around my birthday, he would do malicious things to hurt my feelings, and I noticed he got a rise out of upsetting me. One situation I recall vividly was when he attempted to have someone he was crushing on, sing for me on my birthday. The girl was so defensive and disrespectful when I called her out and told her to keep her gesture to herself. Her serenade was not something I was interested in, and I found it quite sick in the head for someone to do this to someone they "love." I took our daughter and spent my birthday in Colorado Springs without him and with his family. This was just a few days after we all had a lovely time celebrating Christmas in onesie pajamas as a family. His family. He was always doing too much, and I hoped he did what he needed to while I was away. 2015 was another wild year, but it would also be our last.

Chapter 10
The Beginning of The End

The time was drawing near for him to cash out on his settlement from the car accident. He had me on another unnecessary wild emotional rollercoaster. One minute he was so loving, and the other moments, were just pure hell with him. I started to check out mentally. There was no regard for how I felt about anything, he didn't include me in anything he was doing, and if he did, he would find a reason not to let me be a part of it.

I remember thinking about divorce and grieving the entire process in my head. He would catch me crying, thinking he was hurting my feelings, when I was just building up the courage and plan to leave him. I would always tell him, "If this is what you call love, I would hate to see what hate looks like coming from you." We tried counseling, but again, he felt he didn't need help. He said I was the one who needed help. I questioned him one day, "how can you need a person you don't like so much? Why are you still here if I'm such a bad, evil person?" I wasn't doing anything to this man for him to feel this way besides challenging him to do better, as he felt on top of the world and above the law.

He spent a lot of time with the neighbors. Sometimes in the middle of our hangout as a family, he would get up and go across the street and come home after spending a short while over there.

The Truth is a Lie

We were all cool. The neighbor heard that I could rap, and he was invited over by the Manipulative Deceiver to hear my flow. I spit something for him, and he wanted me to feature on a song called "Money Maker Move" as he and his people were getting ready to do a show at the "Cassidy" Concert. Since we were married, this was the first time I would showcase my musical talent.

We did the show, and the turnout was successful. One of my good girlfriends, who was in support of me when my grandmother passed away, came, and we had a ball. The Manipulative Deceiver was "feeling himself" as he had just come into the settlement payout from the car accident. He bought everyone who came out to support a shot at the bar and left my friend out. I didn't drink because I was nursing. I didn't find this out until later, but I've seen with my own eyes how he would treat her when she came by. Sometimes he would attempt to shut the door in her face on her way inside. He was cold towards her during this time, and he couldn't stand that I had her support.

After he received his settlement money, I made it a point not to dictate how he should spend it. He was sure he could provide as a "man," and I was curious how he would pull this off without having any money management skills. I didn't want conflict, so I let him do what he wanted. He attempted to buy me a car, and I didn't want it. Any gift he purchased for me in the past was either used or something more useful for him, and I didn't want him to attempt to throw this "act of kindness" in my face or take it back in a fit of pettiness. He purchased the display Rolland Motif keyboard for me, and I immediately took it to my brother's house when things worsened.

Around April or May of 2016, we barely spoke. My oldest son became rebellious and ran away to be with his father. The Manipulative Deceiver was in and out of the house as he pleased and heavily in the company of his male friends. I never got a break. My emotional needs were unmet, and all I could think of was, "he's only treating me like this because he's resentful about the burn." I figured he was out in the streets cheating, ashamed of exposing his scars and constantly reminded of me while he was doing God knows what.

I heard rumors of him being at bars with women while I was at home with the children, trying to run my program out of the church. I informed our church about what we were dealing with and threatened to leave because of the emotional and alcohol abuse I was experiencing with him. When I challenged the pastor that scripture wasn't helpful in our situation because we weren't living by the law of the book, I was asked to leave the church, and I never returned. My business was taken off the referral list. My self-esteem was shot; I was breaking and unemployed with a husband who refused to keep our children long enough for me to go on interviews.

The Truth is a Lie

My baby boy was about 9 months old, and I was still nursing. Already depressed and down, the Manipulative Deceiver comes home upset. He thought I would get caught up in his emotions, but I ignored him. He accused me of cheating, saying our youngest baby wasn't his and making statements about how I burned him on purpose. I was hurt because now my feelings were confirmed; as much as I wanted to be right about things, this was something I was hoping to be wrong about. Hearing him say that took me out of character, and I became defensive. The fact that he came home mad for no reason to pick a fight made me think he was projecting what he was doing to me behind closed doors. And I couldn't think of why he would think I would want to hurt him intentionally.

After about twenty minutes of dealing with his random tantrum, he asked me for the money he gave me to get my nails done about four days before this incident, and I handed it to him. He looked me in the eyes, threw the money in my face, and ordered me to pick it up. I was shocked. I couldn't believe he would do something like that and for what reason? I looked at the money on the ground and then up at him and said, "did that make you feel like a man?" He picked the money up off the floor, threw the money in my face again, and said, "Money Maker Move, right?" Inside, I was feeling like outing this man's lights. But I got a hold of my emotions and walked away. He stormed out of the house and left with the car.

INDY GOHARD

When he left, I began to feel anger, sadness, and, most of all, hopelessness. I thought about how we could end our relationship peacefully, and confused that if he hated me so much, why didn't he just leave? Things were getting worse between us after he got this money, and the sad part is I expected it to happen. I believe that my lack of emotion toward how he was treating me confused the hell out of him because he was also trying to find a way out but didn't have the courage to just leave without finding a way to do it without being the "bad guy".

He was gone for about two hours, and I had an interview lined up that day, but he left with the car and turned his phone off so I wouldn't make it. I thought about all the mistakes I made in the marriage and attempted to take my own life months before this. I remember a few things about the incident. One of my good girlfriends was there to support me. Before she arrived, the nurse pulled up my emergency contact and read off my deceased grandmother. I remember finally bawling my eyes out because her wisdom was what I needed right then. At this time, her passing became very real to me, and I sobbed uncontrollably. They went down the line of my next of kin and contacted the Manipulative Deceiver. When he got to the hospital, he was drunk and brought three of my children up there with him. He placed our baby on my chest, who had been crying and ready to nurse. He called me selfish, told me I was attention-seeking, and argued with the security guard in front of the hospital and my friend before he was asked to leave the building. After leaving, he also went to my brother's house and gossiped about my mental breakdown. I was diagnosed with postpartum depression and asked if I needed to stay for monitoring, but I decided to be released to my friend and return home to my children.

I stayed away from church and dove into spirituality. This started to come back to myself slowly but surely. He didn't like that either. His image was everything. He was concerned that other people thought there had to be bigger issues going on if wifey wasn't going to church. Out of curiosity, I burned sage to see what it would do and twice after I burned it, he was at the house in the driveway asleep in his car and never came inside.

The last straw was in July 2016. We got into a huge argument. Again, I was concerned about this mental state and in fear for my life at this point because not only was he in and out of the house as he pleased, but he would bust in our room door to scare me. When he left, he would create rumors saying I was trying to kill him. My neighbor would come by asking if things were okay as he would go cry to them and come home like nothing happened. This night, I locked myself in the room with our baby, and our daughter was in her bed across from us. He was in the music room next door. I heard him talking loudly as if someone else was there with him. When I opened the door, he was in the room holding our daughter and talking recklessly about me when I thought he was alone the entire time. I grabbed my daughter out of the room and began recording him with my phone.

He comes busting in the door after I got my footage, comes over to the side of the bed and grabs my phone off the floor, deleting all my material. He didn't know he started recording himself, though. The video captures him saying, "We're going to do it live," with his face facing the camera. You could hear me say, "give me back my phone or I will bleach your pants. Give me my phone, even trade, and I won't do it." He antagonized me until I got the courage to splash the bleach on his pants, and after this, the video shut off.

My phone was thrown to the floor, and he physically attacked me in front of my children, choking me on the bed next to my 9-month-old baby. Our daughter was so used to us arguing she didn't even bat an eye at what her father was doing. When I started losing consciousness, he fell to the ground in a fetal position and began to cry as if he wanted me to feel sorry for him. It was so weird. I grabbed my babies and my phone and ran out of the house to call the police. When the police arrived, I was still standing outside. They walked inside to take his statement after they took mine, and when they came out, the officers were going to place me under arrest because he suddenly had missing hair in the front and scratches on his face.

The Truth is a Lie

The funny thing was, I never laid a hand on him. When I explained the situation, the police said one of us had to leave, and I chose to go since I was the one without anything. I felt like I had no right to be in my own home, and I had no fight left in me. I wasn't even fighting for myself. Over the next seven days, I would spend my days in pain from being so engorged from milk, with no pump and no baby.

I was gone for about a week. When I returned home, he was cleaning out the house. I had a different walk about me. I don't know, but something about that experience repurposed me, and I felt empowered. When I got to the door, loud jazz music was playing, and he was standing outside looking like he was getting ready for company to come over or something. I looked at him and said, the next time you put your hands on me, I'm going to kill you, and I walked inside the house to my babies. He immediately called his family and told them I threatened to kill him again for no reason. There was a reason. He knew what it was, and if he and I knew, that's all that mattered to me.

Chapter 11
The Great Escape

On September 4, 2016, I filed for divorce. My baby turned 1 year a month prior, and the Manipulative Deceiver told friends and family that he couldn't live with me because I was trying to ruin his life and tried to kill him. God knows I barely said anything to him besides what I needed to say. I felt like I was on the top of a rollercoaster, anticipating the descent. I was nervous because I had no support for my children to help me get a job interview, and they were not old enough that I could leave them at home alone.

He took the car that was supposed to be mine. I took the car we shared together and traded it for a 2016 Chevy Cruz brand new with only 13 miles. My credit was so good they only asked for the application and my last employer. I got lucky. I was able to get rid of the other car, which was a "death trap" and the only piece of debt we owned together. He was pissed and confused about how I was able to pull this off when we were trying to purchase nicer cars together in the past and was unsuccessful. He should have been happy we no longer shared an obligation, which was one less thing to itemize.

Fast forward to October 17, 2016, he sent me a text message saying he was leaving and not coming back. That evening, he came home, and I asked him what I was supposed to do. Before he chose

The Truth is a Lie

to leave, we decided when we would split, we would do it in a way that wouldn't leave either one of us in financial ruin. This time, he told me I needed to figure it out. I later found out he recorded bits and pieces of our conversations, specifically times when he aggravated me for a reaction and played it back to anyone who would listen. The next day he showed up with a U-Haul and a couple of his friends and took everything from electronics, beds, my oldest son's video game collection, CDs, the children's social security cards, birth certificates, the children's toys, clothes, and anything I could use to get any financial help. He asked for my keyboard, and he never got it back because it was at my brother's house. Although they were cool, my brother wouldn't let him have it.

A couple of days later, I found out from our landlord that October's rent was never paid. He left me in the house without money or resources, and the rent was due. On October 20th, I was driving down the highway headed to sell my keyboard, and I got a call from a temp agency asking if I came to interview with them within the next hour, they would get me in as soon as Monday. I was so excited! My prayers were finally being answered! The company was looking to fill a position until the end of December, and I was ready. I still needed to pay the rent, so I sold the keyboard for 900 dollars, and one of my relatives moved in and covered the rest.

During mediation, he was accompanied by a young lady. I explained to the mediator that it would make sense for him to move on with his life and visit when he could since that's what he was doing anyways. Court was the last thing I wanted to go back into since I already knew what to expect. The idea was to avoid the courts from making a decision that was least favorable to any of us. I wished for him to get well and work on himself, but he still wanted to fight and swore I wanted to keep our children from him. Here we go again! After hearing his side, the mediator agreed with me and my proposal to the court, which was completely fair. While he was out of the house, he said, "if I can't have my children, nobody can." And did everything in his power to make my life miserable and difficult with this process. He said he wanted a divorce, but his actions were sabotaging it. Earlier that year, before he received the settlement, we started a life insurance policy for our family, which totaled three hundred thousand dollars. We took out this amount intending to be ahead of the game in hopes of purchasing our home together.

Our divorce case was being handled in Adams County court. The mediation was never considered at our divorce hearing since he contested the agreement, and my claim of domestic violence was ignored. I came up with a different approach this time. In my response to the issues the Manipulative Deceiver brought forth in court, I immediately requested to have a guardian ad litem, and I asked the courts for help. I didn't go bashing him at all, but I did speak the truth. The judge in our divorce wanted this one to be open

The Truth is a Lie

and shut. He dismissed my claim of domestic violence against him due to a lack of character witnesses, gave me primary physical custody and shared decision-making. According to former judge Salcido, judges are supposedly trained to be concerned about the time domestic violence is brought up. My domestic claim was made in the beginning, and it was ignored.

After it was all said and done, he was ordered to pay over 900 in child support, and he owed my dad a total of 1 thousand dollars. Before this, I told the judge I didn't want child support or alimony, but child support was granted to me by law due to the number of days I had the children. To put the icing on the cake, he gave the Manipulative Deceiver the three-hundred-thousand-dollar life insurance policy since it was in his name. the settlement money was gone, and he now has access to a three-hundred-thousand-dollar policy without three-hundred-thousand-dollar worth of negative assets. The Judge also told me he wasn't required to return the documents he took despite me having the children primarily. He told me if I needed new social security documents and birth certificates, I needed to order another set separately, which was financially inconveniencing and time-consuming. After hearing the judgment, my mouth dropped, and so did his. He left the courtroom crying, and so did I. I cried because I knew this was far from over. I think he cried because he knew what he would put me through. I took care of him all our marriage, and now he is ordered to pay me. I knew it wouldn't end well, and I was sure the courts just set this case up for murder.

For the next three years, the Manipulative Deceiver called the police on me over one hundred times for claims of me not giving him his children, false child abuses and neglect claims, stalking, harassing, and recording my reactions after deliberately antagonizing me. I kept the children until the insurance policy was scheduled to be due again because I knew he would have to let it lapse, considering his new financial situation. And it did. I knew as long as I feared for my children's safety and it was legit, which it was, there was nothing the courts could do. But they sure tried it.

The cycle with the court continued. I wouldn't let up, and I wouldn't give up. This man tried to duplicate the efforts of the Bitter Deceiver and did a damn good job at it too. His entire "smear campaign" was more concerned with helping save his image than encouraging him to get help. My biggest issue was his willingness to put our children and myself in danger for the sake of proving a point. On times he did have the kids, he would drop them off when he wasn't supposed to be driving, under the influence, and they were not in car seats. Each time I complained about it to the court, it was dismissed. Each motion I filed was a waste of time. Again, we had no representation. He would bring different women to our hearings and perjure the court with false accusations. I learned that when he was supposed to be exercising his parenting time, he would leave

The Truth is a Lie

our children alone with his girlfriend I barely knew instead of just letting them stay home. My daughter would claim his girlfriend wasn't feeding them unless their father was home. She was also not the same woman that attended mediation in the beginning. He didn't let anyone cause any harm to these children but him! He knew the difference between right and wrong; because of this, I didn't play with his ass or court either. Not this time.

The three years in court was pure hell. He was telling our children I didn't want him to be with them, but he was leaving them with his girlfriend on his parenting time, and when it was time to return them, he would make a fuss that he wasn't getting enough time. The children would cry when it was time to return home to me, and he would tell them, "mommy doesn't want us to be together," He was attempting to build a case to have the courts change the existing agreement. He didn't realize that if he weren't a danger to himself or anyone else, we wouldn't be in this situation, to begin with. This had nothing to do with me controlling the situation aside from the fact I was protecting my children, and he was still attempting to control how my time was spent by using the courts to abuse me. It is a dangerous game when you are going against someone who is keeping up an image; even more so, someone who is paid for their image because that's their means of survival.

I began to lose my hair, and complete faith in the system. That's gone. Despite my claims of all that was happening, I took the escalated issues to every court in the courthouse. We were in criminal court, restraining order court, and family court. None of them wanted any responsibility or ties to potential lawsuits, so they dismissed every claim I made. He was lying about his substance abuse and mental health issues.

Funny how a family court is treated like a criminal court, but for some reason, we don't get public defenders in that branch of the court. We need a team of attorneys defending this public group and psychological professionals who can diagnose mental issues because it's needed for public safety. We go to court to find a solution but we leave with justice unserved. Without legal representation and professionals who could get a deeper look at motives and mental capacities, cases are extended unnecessarily to keep them in rotation. They don't give a fuck about us. We are expected to go in without emotion which is nearly impossible. Being in family court is like watching your babies drown and being punished for trying to save them.

I provided the two examples not only to raise awareness of what went on behind closed doors but because there is no way any loving parent can go into court fully represented or by themselves, knowing that their ex is dealing with mental or substance abuse issues, be called hyper-vigilant, treated like the bitter ex, and nobody is held accountable. But this happens, and it happens often. There is something wrong here.

The Truth is a Lie

I have records of the court's biased statements about me in the final orders. The burden of proof always ended up with me in motions that I filed. This made no sense. Again, there is no due process in family court. He was so good a fooling the courts and getting them to show him a favor when he was completely out of line and unsafe. For prestigious people with degrees and certifications, they were unskilled at detecting someone under the influence of substances as he regularly did. Do you know why? Because they are not trained to do so. Leave that to the mental professionals. I would call it out, and they would call me a liar. Scary shit.

In the end, I followed the law as best as possible but still withheld my children despite what they said. In May 2019, I filed a restraining order on the Manipulative Deceiver, which was ultimately dropped, but on record, they found the issue of domestic violence that occurred in 2016. The same one that was disregarded at my initial divorce hearing which would have changed the entire trajectory of our divorce initially. I also filed a motion to relocate, and I told Judge Caryn Datz I was taking my children no matter the outcome. At this point, without my children, I had nothing to lose but my job and my mind.

A month later, I gave the children to his parents while I went to find a place in Nevada. When I returned to Colorado, I was contacted by child protective services as he was pulled over on the highway for reckless driving. He was drinking and driving with my children and his nephew in the car, but they were not in their car seats. Look at God! He was caught doing the very thing I went to court complaining about for the past three years! Even with this new evidence, I was still treated poorly by the courts, told the jurisdiction would remain in Colorado, and they still allowed him to have split decision-making knowing we were unable to co-parent due to his abusive behavior, which is a factor that goes against a child's best interest. The truth was revealed but still treated as a lie. After the hearing, the court allowed me to relocate with my children under strict stipulations before the Judge condescendingly told me to have a great life and before solidifying her orders with the final hit of the gavel. I followed the rules in the motion to relocate, and there was nothing they could do but let me leave. Three years fast forward, and the Manipulative Deceiver entered a treatment facility for two years. Here's the deal, once he's finished, the allegations he had against our children go away like they never happened. I was never notified about the status of the hearings our children were involved in. Why is that Colorado? This sounds like a deferred adjudication to me. This is a type of plea bargain a defendant can take where they can complete certain requirements ordered by the court to avoid a conviction on their record. Regardless, I still have a legal right and duty to protect my children from any known danger and will continue to do so by all means necessary.

The Truth is a Lie

Side notes

Restraining orders can hinder and make visitations complicated and, in some cases, non-existent. When children are involved, judges are apprehensive and take greater caution before permanently restraining parties in domestic disputes. They do not stop an offender from offending you. It's just a piece of paper that says, "this person is legally not allowed to be around you," and legal action can be taken against the perpetrator if you can provide evidence of a violation. It doesn't prevent you from future offenses, third parties, or even in worse cases, death. It's only good for documentation purposes. That's it. Here are three words… What's the point?

Growing up, I lived in toxicity with people who had mental illnesses, substance abuse issues, and personality disorders. My grandmother allowed it, and on the flip side, the knowledge of it permitted me to recognize how careful these people need to be handled. The outcome of forcing a co-parenting agreement with people who have these issues can be extremely detrimental to a child and their parent.

For example, my willingness to heal others through compassion and empathy has caused me a lot of heartaches, starting with my own mother. She would come home from her drug binges and promise us she would stop. She also made us emotionally responsible for her bullshit. My mom would go to treatment and rehab programs. None of them worked. She would guarantee us and beg for our grace and mercy to have patience with her. Treatment was only a priority when it was court-ordered, but when it was all done, she returned to do the same things she was doing before. There was a time when she took my brother and me to court as "props" in hopes they would have leniency on her for whatever she did, and they still sent her to jail. We had to call our grandmother to let her know we were stranded at the courthouse and needed a ride home. The effects of dealing with this all my life left me detached at one point. It got so bad I felt uncomfortable showing my children affection out of fear of getting too connected to them, and in case they departed from me, I wouldn't be so broken. They knew that I loved them in other ways.

From an early age, I was able to see how the system didn't and still doesn't work. I should know how it should work from being in it. I was blessed with wonderful social workers but without people like them, the system is still broken. To this day, my mother still has problems with substances, and when I give her an opportunity to talk to me after so long, she doesn't hesitate to remind me that I "snitched on her" to her probation officer for not following court orders when I was about twelve years old. I am a grown woman now! What a statement from a person who says they love their children. My mother, the woman who was supposed to be fighting for us to be in her custody, is still mad at me for calling her probation officer, this way, she could get the help she needed and not end up dead in the street. She wasn't there on the nights that her mother would have us pray for her safety and well-being. She doesn't remember the times she put up with dealing with her narcissistic behavior. My mother swore my grandma was trying to keep us away from her when she was keeping herself away from us. One thing is for certain people with a hard time processing accountability, or following rules have one thing in common; a parent who enables their behavior. "I'm sorry grandma. Had to say it."

I see how this all repeated itself in my personal dealings with men. I enabled and allowed a lot of mess to unfold in my personal relationships to avoid conflict, not realizing that just because I put the blanket over my head doesn't mean the monster can't get me. In relation to the two dynamics, I would do things to keep my mom's attention in hopes she wouldn't disappear again. I blamed myself for not being able to keep her home to raise us. My childhood trauma was "people pleasing" and "over excelling" because I knew it brought my family honor. I became overly independent because of the notion that my mother was sick and needed my help. I wanted to be the one who saved her. But when I had my own child at the age of 16, it clicked that the person who needed rescuing was me.

The Bitter Deceiver and the Manipulative Deceiver both

have issues deeper than they're willing to admit. Some of them, I found out about later. I'm sure there are things I still don't know. Truly, you never know a person until you live with them. You see sides, that family and friends don't see. They con their way through the system using loopholes to either shorten or terminate their obligation to the courts. The assigned public officials overlook important details and quickly move on to the next case. There is way too much convolution for a single solution. Not only that, but courts also receive grants and taxpayer money to keep this shit in rotation.

Prolonged exposure to trauma can cause mental illnesses, and most of us in the African American community have been exposed to so much unhealed trauma due to a lack of resources and the stigma of being shamed or labeled "crazy" amongst peers. Psychiatry.org reports only one-in-three African Americans who need mental health care, receive it. The key word is "need." Most people with mental health issues, especially men within this community, do not want to admit they need help. Then we add our hopeful but ignorant hindsight, mix that with other unhealed people, typically those with similar childhood traumas, bond, and breed with them. What a recipe for disaster.

One day, we'll smarten up, perhaps create our own programs and systems, and develop the emotional intelligence to put our babies first and handle our own affairs because the system as we know it will never be accountable. Our children are our

The Truth is a Lie

responsibility at the end of the day, and these public officials get to go home to their families at night while we suffer in silence, trying to keep ourselves and our babies from dying at the hands of people who are skilled at using the system to abuse us. In the sight of the court, we are a job for them. That's it. Bitter and Manipulative people are aware of this. They know if they could use their charm, create clever narratives, and bypass public officials who are not on their jobs, the cycle will continue, and we're back in the system as a new case number which most likely will not be a case number from the family court.

Final Thoughts

- Judge Caryn Datz, not that you genuinely care, but my children are doing much better, and we are living great lives. I purchased them a big home one year after your decision, and they are happy and thriving. I hope my book finds you in good spirits.

- Bonnie Saltzman, because of your expert advice to the court and me being the bigger person still when I moved on with my life again, the Bitter Deceiver and his family used everything I went through and turned my child against me. This was also a concern of mine eight years ago when I told you he was trying to do this. I tried to give the benefit of the doubt, but only a psychiatrist can diagnose mental illness. Not people without clinical certifications. I would love to see an audit of your cases take place. You also had a case that occurred in 2018, and the person was living in my home. You never interviewed me as someone who cared for that child in my home, but you made sure to let your client know; I knew you very well. That is definitely misconduct.

- Public officials of the entire judicial system, your power is in integrity and relational intelligence. It takes a high level of discernment and relational intellect to get up and work on behalf of "the people." Remember that before making decisions that negatively affect innocent citizens. Especially children and children with caring custodial parents. There is a reason we are the way we

The Truth is a Lie

are, and that part is not programmed in your training.

- To my baby girl, who I no longer see or hear from, I have done everything I know to do. Some things may not have been the best choices, but I did what I thought was best for you and your siblings in all situations. I do not love you any less than the others. You are, and forever will be, a part of me. I apologize for any hurt you may have experienced with all our chaos, and I want you to know that none of this is your fault. Sometimes I was not emotionally available to you because I didn't know how to be. I ask that you find it in your heart someday to forgive me. I love you forever and always will.

- Protective parents, don't stop talking. Don't stop fighting, and keep all your evidence together as best as you can. Stay away from people who make you question your reality. If you're experiencing domestic abuse, tell someone, record, keep all your important documents closed and plan as best as you can. Write it down if you have no one to turn to, but don't stay silent.

National Domestic Hotline 800-799-7233
Suicide and Crisis Hotline – Dial or SMS 988

About the Author

Indy GoHard is the proud mother of four children. She obtained a bachelor's degree in Criminal Justice with a specialized focus in Juvenile Justice. As a former foster youth, she took advantage of the resources the state had to offer as a step up, and because of the value it proved all her life, she became an advocate for children after having her fourth child. She is a speaker, author, and life coach.

www.ingramcontent.com/pod-product-compliance
Lightning Source LLC
Chambersburg PA
CBHW070244220526
45465CB00004B/1519